Contemporary

Asian

Architects

Hasan-Uddin Khan

Contemporary
Asian
Architects

TASCHEN

KÖLN LISBOA LONDON NEW YORK OSAKA PARIS

Dedication · Widmung · Dédicace

To Karen R. Longeteig with love and thanks for her support, help and forbearance with my erratic lifestyle over the last twenty years.

Für Karen R. Longeteig in Liebe und Dankbarkeit für ihre Unterstützung und Hilfe, ihre Geduld und Nachsicht mit meinem unsteten Lebensstil während der letzten zwanzig Jahre.

A Karen R. Longeteig avec mon affection et mes remerciements pour ses encouragements, son aide et sa patience envers mon style de vie fantasque durant ces vingt dernières années.

Page 2 · Seite 2
Kyu Sung Woo Architect: Olympic Village Housing (1988), Seoul, courtyard of the curved galleria
Photo: © Mick Hales

This book was printed on 100% chlorine-free bleached paper in accordance with the TCF-standard.

© 1995 Benedikt Taschen Verlag GmbH
Hohenzollernring 53, D-50672 Köln

Cover Design: Angelika Muthesius, Cologne; Mark Thomson, London
Design: Frank Schwab, Schwäbisch Gmünd
Project Management: Silvia Krieger, Cologne
French translation: Annie Berthold, Düsseldorf
German translation: Sabine Buken, Berlin

Printed in Italy
ISBN 3-8228-8670-X

Contents
Inhalt
Sommaire

Asian Architecture:
Diversity and Eclecticism

Architektur in Asien:
Vielfalt und Eklektizismus

L´architecture asiatique:
diversité et éclectisme

Robert L. Miller

Architecture in Asia has altered dramatically since the mid-1940s when most of the countries on the continent achieved independence. The rate of change has been unprecedented and the scale of development is daunting, making the past decades a fertile period for Asian architects in nations where new architecture and new roles for professionals are demanded. While it is true that many Asian countries are poor and that the majority of their populations live in sub-standard conditions, economic growth in the past decades has led to a reassessment of the potential inherent in these societies, many of which play significant regional and international roles. Introducing this emerging and rapidly eventful story is a challenge. My approach, which is illustrative of certain major concerns and tendencies rather than comprehensive, consists of presenting a selection of contemporary ideas, projects, and people – a glimpse into a diverse Asian world from both historical and thematic viewpoints.

The area with which we are concerned stretches from Turkey in the west, through the Arab world and the Indo-Pakistani sub-continent, to the South-east Asian states and the archipelago in the east – all of which have cultures influenced in varying degrees by Islam since the 7th century, sometimes as an overlay on Hinduism and other religions. To the north lies the great giant China, flanked by the "four little dragons" – Hong Kong, South Korea, Taiwan, and Singapore – and the islands of Japan, all influenced by the Confucian, Buddhist, and Taoist traditions. Also included are Buddhist Thailand, Burma, and the mostly Christian Philippines. In the past century they have all been the focus of external forces, either under colonialist domination or influenced and changed by Western interventions, trade, and models of development.

The prevalence of such external forces has conditioned the paradigm of development and thinking in many ways. Witness the importance of political leaders and professionals engaged in "liberation" struggles, and the use of the term "Third World" in reply to descriptions coined in the West such as "underdeveloped", "developing" and, more recently, "lesser developed" and "less advantaged". The Third World label originated at the 1952 Bandung Confer-

Seit der Mitte der vierziger Jahre, als die meisten Länder des Kontinents ihre Unabhängigkeit erhielten, hat sich die Architektur Asiens ganz entscheidend gewandelt. Eine derart rasante Veränderung hatte es zuvor nicht gegeben. Das Ausmaß dieser Entwicklung ist überwältigend – ein Umstand, der die letzten Jahrzehnte für die Architekten Asiens zu einer sehr fruchtbaren Zeit gemacht hat, ganz besonders in den Ländern, in denen eine neue Art von Architektur und ein neues Rollenverständnis innerhalb der akademischen Berufe gefragt ist. Zwar trifft es zu, daß viele Länder Asiens arm sind, und daß die Mehrheit der dortigen Bevölkerung unterhalb des durchschnittlichen Lebensstandards lebt, doch das in den letzten Jahrzehnten eingetretene Wirtschaftswachstum hat zu einer Neubewertung des in diesen Gesellschaften liegenden Potentials geführt, von denen viele regional wie auch international eine wichtige Rollen spielen. Diese neue, ereignisreiche, ja stürmische Entwicklung einmal vorzuführen, stellt eine herausfordernde Aufgabe dar.

Das Gebiet, mit dem wir uns hier befassen, erstreckt sich von der Türkei im Westen, über die arabische Welt und den indisch-pakistanischen Subkontinent, bis hin zu den südostasiatischen Ländern und den Inselgruppen im Osten – alles Länder, deren Kulturen seit dem siebten Jahrhundert unterschiedlich stark vom Islam beeinflußt worden sind, zuweilen auch in Form einer Überlagerung des Hinduismus oder anderer Religionen. Im Norden liegen das großmächtige China, flankiert von den »vier kleinen Tigern« – Hongkong, Südkorea, Taiwan, Singapur – sowie die japanischen Inseln – sie alle wurden von konfuzianischen, buddhistischen und taoistischen Traditionen geprägt. Auch das buddhistische Thailand, Burma und die überwiegend christlichen Philippinen gehören dazu. Alle diese Länder standen im letzten Jahrhundert im Zentrum auswärtiger Machtinteressen und befanden sich entweder unter kolonialistischer Herrschaft oder unterlagen dem Einfluß bzw. der Veränderung durch westliche Interventionen, Handels- oder Entwicklungsmodelle. Das Vorherrschen dieser äußeren Kräfte bildete in vielerlei Hinsicht die Grundlage für bestimmte Entwicklungs- und Denkmuster. Man denke nur an die Bedeutung der politischen Füh-

L'architecture asiatique s'est modifiée radicalement depuis le milieu des années 40, à partir du moment où la plupart des pays du continent asiatique eurent accédé à l'indépendance. La vitesse des mutations a été sans précédent et l'ampleur du développement impressionnante. Les dernières décennies ont été une période fertile pour les architectes asiatiques dans des pays à la recherche d'une architecture nouvelle et de nouveaux rôles pour les professionnels. Beaucoup de pays restent pauvres, mais la croissance économique des décennies passées a conduit à une réévaluation du potentiel de ces sociétés, dont certaines jouent même maintenant un rôle sur la scène régionale ou internationale. Présenter cette histoire en pleine émergence et riche en événements relève du défi. Je chercherai donc davantage à illustrer certaines questions et tendances majeures de l'architecture asiatique qu'à en dresser un catalogue complet.

L'aire géographique dont il est question s'étend de la Turquie jusqu'à l'archipel de l'Asie du Sud-Est en passant par le monde arabe et le sous-continent indien; toutes ces régions ont été influencées à divers degrés par l'islam depuis le VIIe siècle, ce dernier s'étant parfois superposé à l'hindouisme et aux autres religions. Au Nord, se trouve le grand voisin, la Chine, flanqué des «quatre petits dragons» – Hong Kong, Corée du Sud, Taïwan et Singapour – et des îles du Japon, tous sous l'influence du confucianisme, du bouddhisme et du taoïsme. Cette région comprend aussi la Thaïlande et la Birmanie bouddhistes et les Philippines catholiques. Au siècle dernier, tous ces pays ont subi la domination de puissances extérieures sous des formes diverses: colonialisme, intervention militaire étrangère, commerce, modèles de développement occidentaux.

La prédominance de ces forces extérieures a conditionné de plusieurs manières le modèle de développement et de pensée de ces régions. En témoignent l'importance des leaders politiques et des professionnels engagés dans les luttes de libération ainsi que l'invention du terme «Tiers-Monde» en réponse aux clichés véhiculés en Occident tels que «sous-développé», «en développement» ou, plus récemment encore, «moins développé» et «moins avantagé». Ce terme de «Tiers-Monde», lancé par Nehru,

The low-rise, high-density city developed over time characterizes Asian cities like Jakarta.

Die flach gebaute, dicht besiedelte Stadt, wie sie sich im Laufe der Jahre entwickelt hat, ist für asiatische Städte wie Jakarta typisch.

Djakarta est le type même de la ville asiatique tant par la densité que par la hauteur limitée de ses constructions.

ence by Nehru, Nasser, Tito, Sukarno, and other founders of the Non-Aligned Movement to denote a third path, away from the First World (capitalistic Western) and the Second World (communist), to establish a different identity for the new "emerging worlds", which soon also encompassed South America. Although a politically shrewd idea at the time, the term has lost its significance, and the countries within its sphere have altered beyond recognition, with differing attitudes toward "progress" and different approaches to their physical, economic and cultural realities. Notions of "underdevelopment" and "Third World" are being challenged. The terms, however, continue to be used in lieu of adequate alternatives.

The issue of identity is one that percolated down from the political realm into that of architecture. The questions "Where do we come from? What are we? Where are we going" (to use the title of one of Gauguin's finest paintings) were translated into forms related to specific cultures, religions, or nation-states. The idea that architecture is a reflection of culture remains a strong one and continues to be debated. It is a theme that inspires and constrains the best Asian architects, who return to their roots time and again, albeit in very different ways.

The cities of Asia are changing with speed and turbulence. The models developed in the West – standards, technologies, and notions of progress – have been broadly applied to Asian countries, creating undesirable tensions between realities and ideals. On a cultural level, a great diversity continues to exist in sub-cultures, ethnicity, and regional variations, but the media, multi-national companies and organizations, communications, transport, industrial technology, and trade engender the influence of global culture. The differences between the local or regional, and the international or universal, are becoming more difficult to distinguish. The "authenticity" of place is now tempered by the global, and the architect has to function within this sphere of ambiguity. Although the debate around the need for an authentic regional or national architecture eventually assumed an important place within the architectural discourse, it remains an unresolved issue.

The nature of development and the role of the profes-

rungsschichten und Intellektuellen, die an den »Befreiungskämpfen« beteiligt waren sowie an den Gebrauch des Begriffs »Dritte Welt« als einer Reaktion auf vom Westen geprägte Begriffe wie »unterentwickelt«, »Entwicklungs-...« und seit neuestem auch »weniger entwickelt« oder »unterpriviligiert«. Dieses Dritte-Welt-Etikett war ursprünglich auf der Konferenz von Bandung im Jahre 1952 eingeführt worden, die von Nehru, Nasser, Tito, Sukarno und anderen Begründern der Bewegung der Blockfreien abgehalten worden war, um einen Dritten Weg zu bezeichnen, weg von der Ersten Welt (der kapitalistischen westlichen) und der Zweiten Welt (der kommunistischen), um für die neu »sich konstituierenden Welten«, zu denen bald auch Lateinamerika zählte, eine andere Identität zu schaffen. Obgleich dies damals, politisch gesehen, eine kluge Idee war, hat der Begriff doch an Bedeutung verloren; und die zu dieser Sphäre gehörenden Länder haben sich inzwischen so stark verändert, daß sie kaum mehr wiederzuerkennen sind, mit ihren unterschiedlichen Haltungen gegenüber dem »Fortschritt« und ihrem unterschiedlichen Umgang mit den physischen, ökonomischen und kulturellen Realitäten. Solche Begriffe wie »Unterentwicklung« und »Dritte Welt« werden zwar in Frage gestellt, jedoch, mangels passender Alternativen, weiterhin verwendet.

Die Frage der Identität ist aus der Sphäre des Politischen in die der Architektur »durchgesickert«. Die Fragen: »Woher kommen wir? Was sind wir? Wohin gehen wir?« (um hier den Titel eines der schönsten Bilder Gauguins zu verwenden) haben ihren Niederschlag in Formen gefunden, die einen direkten Bezug zu bestimmten Kulturen, Religionen oder Nationalstaaten haben. Die Vorstellung, daß Architektur eine Widerspiegelung von Kultur ist, inspiriert die besten Architekten Asiens und läßt sie immer wieder zu ihren Wurzeln zurückkehren, wenn auch auf jeweils ganz unterschiedliche Art und Weise.

Die Städte Asiens sind in einer rasanten, ja stürmischen Veränderung begriffen. Die im Westen entwickelten Modelle – Normen, Technologien und Fortschrittsbegriffe – sind zum großen Teil auf die Länder Asiens einfach übertragen worden, was zu unerwünschten Spannungen zwi-

Nasser, Tito, Sukarno et d'autres fondateurs du mouvement des pays non-alignés à la conférence internationale de Bandung en 1952, indiquait une troisième voie par rapport au Premier Monde (l'Occident capitaliste) et au Deuxième Monde (communiste), et cherchait à établir une identité différente pour ces «mondes en émergence» auxquels se joindra un peu plus tard l'Amérique du Sud. Bien que judicieux à l'époque sur le plan politique, le terme a perdu de son sens et les pays concernés ont beaucoup changé; leurs positions face au «progrès» diffèrent notablement, ainsi que leurs approches des réalités physiques, économiques et culturelles. Les notions de «sous-développement» et de «Tiers-Monde» sont remises en question. Les termes ont cependant toujours cours à défaut d'alternatives adéquates.

La question de l'identité est passée du politique à l'architecture. Les questions «D'où venons-nous? Où sommes-nous? Où allons-nous?» (pour reprendre le titre d'un des plus beaux tableaux de Gauguin) furent traduites en des formes liées à des cultures spécifiques, des religions et des états-nations. L'idée selon laquelle l'architecture est le reflet de la culture est toujours répandue et continue d'être l'objet d'un débat. Elle est à la fois une inspiration et une contrainte pour les meilleurs architectes d'Asie qui retournent ainsi maintes fois à leurs racines, même si c'est par des voies différentes.

Les villes asiatiques connaissent une évolution rapide et mouvementée. Les modèles élaborés en Occident – normes, technologies et notions de progrès – ont été largement appliqués à des pays asiatiques, créant ainsi des tensions indésirables entre réalités et idéaux. S'il existe toujours une grande diversité dans les phénomènes culturels locaux, l'ethnicité et les variations régionales, les médias, les multinationales, les communications, les transports, la technologie industrielle et le commerce favorisent la mondialisation de la culture. Les différences entre le local ou le régional et l'international ou l'universel sont de plus en plus floues. L'«authenticité» du lieu est atténuée par le planétaire et l'architecte doit opérer dans cette sphère d'ambiguïté. Bien qu'occupant finalement une place importante dans le discours architectural, la question

sional is relevant to the building of the next century. Given the specifics of place and culture, one might ask, what drives the notion of place, of city or neighbourhood, or indeed, individual dwelling? What is the direction for development – the image, form, organization, and function of the city? Is it the emulation of the mythic modern city – Chicago, New York, or Houston – being built in Riyadh, Bombay, Shanghai, Tokyo, Hong Kong, Singapore, and Jakarta? Is there an alternative model? If there is one, it has not yet been given form. How far can the architect act as a mediator between local and global aspirations given the fundamental ambiguities that exist in Asian societies? The complex reality is expressed in such different ways, even in a single place, that the overlays of influence are hard to distinguish. The dichotomies of regionalism and internationalism, of tradition and modernity, of past and future, are false ones: the age of simultaneous realities is upon us, and their capacity to co-exist in an eclectic and sometimes syncretic manner is a positive trait. Many architects attempt to synthesize the multiple strands of influence with varying degrees of success. The early attempts to be international and "modern" gave way to attempts to be local and "authentic", and we are now seeing the encompassing of many different influences, which has led to a wide degree of experimentation and eclectic expression in architecture.

While foreign architects have had a significant impact on Asian architecture, the works presented here are by indigenous Asian architects. Although these buildings comprise only one aspect of the architectural production, it is one that is important as a counterpoint to the influences that are homogenizing architecture in vastly different societies. Japan, with its vibrant architectural production (already extensively published), has been left out of this reading and, given a limited amount of space, so have countries such as Iraq and the Philippines. In countries such as China, Taiwan, some Arab states, and the Central Asian Republics, recent architecture by indigenous architects has not yet developed to the extent that it has, for example, in India or Malaysia. These countries have also been omitted in the illustration of architects' works.

schen Ideal und Wirklichkeit geführt hat. Wenngleich innerhalb des Diskurses der Architektur die Diskussion über die Notwendigkeit einer authentischen regionalen bzw. nationalen Architektur im Laufe der Zeit einen hohen Stellenwert erhalten hat, liegt hier doch nach wie vor ein ungelöstes Problem.

Obwohl ausländische Architekten einen bedeutenden Einfluß auf die Architektur Asiens ausgeübt haben, so stammen die hier vorgestellten Werke doch von einheimischen, asiatischen Architekten. Und obgleich diese Bauten nur einen bestimmten Aspekt des gesamten architektonischen Schaffens erfassen, ist dieser doch wichtig als ein Gegengewicht gegenüber jenen Einflüssen, die die Architektur dieser so unterschiedlichen Gesellschaften eher zu vereinheitlichen suchen. Japan, mit seiner regen architektonischen Produktivität (wozu es bereits umfassende Publikationen gibt), ist in diesem Beitrag ausgespart worden; und angesichts des nur begrenzt zur Verfügung stehenden Raumes sind auch Länder wie der Irak und die Philippinen nicht mit aufgeführt worden. In solchen Ländern wie China, Taiwan, einigen arabischen Staaten und in den Republiken Zentralasiens hat sich die Baukunst der einheimischen Architekten in letzter Zeit noch nicht in dem Maße entwickelt, wie dies beispielsweise in Indien oder Malaysia der Fall war. Auch diese Länder sind bei der Darstellung der Werke von Architekten weggelassen worden.

Dieser »erste Versuch« soll Aufschluß geben über wichtige Trends und verschiedene Ansätze, und zwar anhand von Projekten, denen eine internationale Bedeutung zukommt und die dem Diskurs der Architektur neue Dimensionen verleihen. Die Auswahl ist mir schwergefallen, und ich habe mich dabei auf meine zwanzigjährigen Reiseerfahrungen und die eingehende Beschäftigung mit Architekten, Architektur und all den damit verbundenen Problemen Afrikas und Asiens gestützt. Es ist enttäuschend festzustellen, wie wenige Architektinnen aus Asien dabei mit ihren Arbeiten vertreten sind, womit nicht gesagt sein soll, daß es nicht einige bedeutende Bauten von Frauen gäbe. Aber angesichts des gesamten architektonischen Schaffens in diesem Jahrhundert war es mir, im Rahmen einer ersten Vorstellung der Architekten Asiens, nicht möglich,

sur la nécessité d'une architecture authentiquement régionale ou nationale reste entière.

La nature du développement et le rôle des professionnels entrent pour beaucoup dans ce que sera la construction du XXIe siècle. Etant donné les particularités de lieu et de culture, on peut se demander ce qui détermine la notion de lieu, de ville ou de voisinage, en fait, de domicile individuel. Et qu'est-ce qui conditionne le développement: l'image, la forme, l'organisation ou la fonction de la ville? L'imitation de la cité moderne mythique (Chicago, New York ou Houston) construite à Riyad, à Bombay, Shanghaï, Tokyo, Hong Kong, Singapour ou Djakarta? Y a-t-il un autre modèle possible? S'il existe, il n'a pas encore pris forme. Jusqu'où l'architecte peut-il être un médiateur entre les aspirations locales et les aspirations universelles, étant donné les ambiguïtés fondamentales des sociétés asiatiques? La réalité dans sa complexité est exprimée de manière tellement différente qu'il est difficile de distinguer les strates d'influence. Les dichotomies régionalisme/internationalisme, tradition/modernité, passé/avenir, sont erronées: notre époque est celle des réalités simultanées, et leur capacité à coexister est un aspect positif. De nombreux architectes essaient de marier les influences, avec des résultats plus ou moins réussis. Auparavant, on cherchait à être international et «moderne». Aujourd'hui, on veut du local et de l'«authentique».

Malgré les nombreuses réalisations des architectes étrangers en Asie les travaux présentés ici sont tous l'œuvre d'architectes autochtones. Ils ne constituent qu'un aspect de la production architecturale, mais un aspect important, puisqu'ils vont à contre-courant de l'homogénéisation qui menace l'architecture. Le Japon, avec son éclatante production architecturale (déjà largement publiée), a été laissé de côté, ainsi que, pour des raisons d'espace, des pays comme l'Irak et les Philippines. En Chine, à Taïwan, dans certains pays arabes et dans les Républiques d'Asie Centrale, l'architecture récente réalisée par des architectes nationaux n'a pas encore atteint le développement de celle de l'Inde ou de la Malaisie, par exemple. Ces pays ont donc été omis eux aussi de ce livre.

Contemporary Asian cities, such as Kuala Lumpur, aspire to the image of American high-rise modernity.

Zeitgenössische asiatische Städte wie Kuala Lumpur orientieren sich am Erscheinungsbild der amerikanischen Moderne mit ihrer Hochhausarchitektur.

Avec leurs hautes constructions, les villes asiatiques contemporaines telles que Kuala Lumpur aspirent à une image de modernité à l'américaine.

The National Library (1976) in Dhaka, Bangladesh,
by Mazharul Islam.

Die National Library (1976) in Dakka, Bangladesch,
von Mazharul Islam.

La National Library (1976) de Mazharul Islam à
Dacca, Bangladesh.

This "first cut" illustrates significant trends and diversity of approaches, with projects that are internationally significant and add new dimensions to the architectural discourse. The choice was a difficult one based on my twenty years of travel and exposure to architects, architecture and related issues in Africa and Asia. It is disappointing to note the paucity of work by women architects in Asia, which is not to say that there are not some significant buildings by women. However, given the sum of architectural production over the century for a first introduction to Asian architects, I was unable to select any women architects for inclusion in this volume, even though projects by architects such as Minnette De Silva of Sri Lanka and Yasmeen Lari of Pakistan achieve distinction. In this vein, the older generation of influential architects such as Mazharul Islam of Bangladesh and Laurie Baker of India, or deceased architects like Hassan Fathy of Egypt, Mehdi Ali Mirza of Pakistan, and Sedad Eldem of Turkey, is not represented in the individual selections.

The roots of contemporary building
Each society and region in Asia has a rich and varied past, which produced magnificent structures such as Borobodur in central Java and the Suleymaniye Mosque in Istanbul, and cities like Mohenjadaro in Pakistan and the Forbidden City in Beijing. The influences of the distant past form the heritage and legacy of these societies. But it is the more recent past, since 19th-century industrialization and mass migration, that largely defined the architecture of contemporary Asian societies, notwithstanding the impact of colonialism since the 17th century with the presence of the British in India and the Dutch in Indonesia. The "Great Game" played by the British and the Russians for the control of Central Asia continued into the 20th century, and the "cold war" between America and the Soviet Union lasted until the late 1980s. Only a few parts of Asia did not fall under direct external control, and there appear to be only minor exceptions in the 20th century where Europe and America have not had a significant impact.

Colonization brought with it the penetration of local and regional institutions, creating situations of confrontation

Student dormitories at Jahangirnagar University
(1968–71) near Dhaka, Bangladesh, by Mazharul
Islam.

Studentenwohnheime, Jahangirnagar University
(1968–71) bei Dakka, Bangladesch, von Mazharul
Islam.

Dortoirs d'étudiants de la Jahangirnagar University
(1968–71) de Mazharul Islam, près de Dacca,
Bangladesh.

in diesen Band auch Architektinnen mit aufzunehmen,
obwohl die Projekte einer Minnette De Silva aus
Sri Lanka und einer Yasmeen Lari aus Pakistan durchaus
gewürdigt werden. Ebenso sind einflußreiche Architekten
der älteren Generation, wie beispielsweise Mazharul
Islam aus Bangladesch und Laurie Baker aus Indien, oder
verstorbene Architekten wie Hassan Fathy aus Ägypten,
Mehdi Ali Mirza aus Pakistan und Sedad Eldem aus der
Türkei, bei dieser Auswahl nicht berücksichtigt worden.

Die Wurzeln zeitgenössischen Bauens
Alle Gesellschaften und Bereiche Asiens weisen eine
reiche und wechselvolle Vergangenheit auf, wodurch so
prachtvolle Bauwerke wie die Tempelanlage von Borobodur im Inneren Javas und die Suleiman Moschee in Istanbul, ebenso Städte wie Mohenjadaro in Pakistan und die
Verbotene Stadt in Peking hervorgebracht wurden. Diese
Einflüsse aus ferner Vergangenheit stellen das Erbe und
das Vermächtnis dieser Gesellschaften dar. Es ist jedoch
eher die jüngere Vergangenheit, die die Architektur der
heutigen Gesellschaften Asiens weitgehend bestimmt hat,
ungeachtet der starken Beeinflussung durch den Kolonia-
lismus seit dem 17. Jahrhundert, mit seiner Präsenz der
Briten in Indien und der Holländer in Indonesien. Das
»Große Spiel«, das die Briten und die Russen zum Zwecke
der Kontrolle Zentralasiens gespielt haben, hat sich bis in
das 20. Jahrhundert fortgesetzt; und der »Kalte Krieg« zwischen Amerika und der Sowjetunion dauerte bis zum Ende
der achtziger Jahre dieses Jahrhunderts. Es gab nur
wenige Teile Asiens, die nicht einer direkten Kontrolle von
außen unterstanden.

Die Kolonisierung brachte eine Durchdringung lokaler
und regionaler Institutionen mit sich, was zu Konfrontatio-
nen zwischen Bestehendem und Neuem führte. Die Kolonisatoren hatten eine ganz andere Art, an die Dinge heran-
zugehen und verfolgten auch andere lang- und kurzfristige
Ziele. Auch ist das Verhältnis zwischen Planungs- und Bauweise der Kolonisatoren und den Kolonisierten keineswegs
unkompliziert. Es ist nicht nur, wie manchmal angenom-
men wird, etwas Aufgezwungenes oder die Imitation des
Baustils der jeweiligen Kolonialmacht, die man in den kolo-

Cette «initiation» illustre les tendances fondamentales
de l'architecture asiatique et la diversité des approches en
présentant des projets d'une portée internationale et qui
apportent une dimension nouvelle au discours architectural. Le choix, qui s'est avéré difficile, est basé sur mon
expérience accumulée au cours de vingt années de
voyage et de pratique des architectes, de l'architecture et
des questions corollaires concernant l'Asie et l'Afrique. On
peut regretter la rareté des œuvres architecturales de
femmes en Asie, ce qui ne veut pas dire, bien entendu,
que certaines n'aient pas réalisé quelques constructions
intéressantes. Vu la production architecturale depuis un
siècle, il m'a pourtant été impossible pour cette introduction à l'architecture asiatique de sélectionner des réalisations de femmes architectes, même si certains projets de
Minnette De Silva du Sri Lanka ou de Yasmeen Lari du
Pakistan sont d'une grande distinction. Pour la même raison, l'ancienne génération – Mazharul Islam du Bangladesh et Laurie Baker d'Inde – ou les architectes disparus –
Hassan Fathy d'Egypte, Mehdi Ali Mirza du Pakistan et
Sedad Eldem de Turquie, ne figurent pas dans la sélection.

Origines de l'architecture contemporaine
Chaque société et région d'Asie a un passé riche et varié
qui a produit des structures magnifiques telles Borobodur,
célèbre stûpa bouddhique du centre de Java, la mosquée
de Soliman à Istanbul, le site archéologique de Mohenjo-
Daro au Pakistan et la «cité interdite» à Pékin. Les
influences d'un lointain passé sont l'héritage de ces sociétés. Mais c'est le passé plus récent, débutant avec l'industrialisation du XIXe siècle et les grandes migrations, qui
définit largement l'architecture des sociétés asiatiques
contemporaines, et ce malgré l'impact du colonialisme –
britannique en Inde et hollandais en Indonésie – à partir du
XVIIe siècle. Le «Grand Jeu» joué par les Britanniques et
les Russes pour prendre le contrôle de l'Asie Centrale per-
dura jusque vers le milieu du XXe siècle, et la «guerre
froide» entre l'Amérique et l'Union Soviétique se prolon-
gea jusque dans les années quatre-vingt. Seules quelques
régions d'Asie échappèrent à la mainmise des grandes
puissances, et rares sont au XXe siècle les pays à n'avoir

between the existing and the new. The colonizers were considerably different in both their approaches and their long- and short-term objectives. Neither is the relationship between the architecture and planning of the colonizers and the colonized straightforward. It is not only, as sometimes perceived, the imposition or imitation of the architecture of the colonizing country that one sees in colonial buildings. In India there was a decision to illustrate not only the might of empire but also the mixing of cultures and tastes of Victorian England with its colony. The monumental architecture of the Edwardian British in India in the 1920s characterized by the imperial structures in New Delhi by Sir Edwin Lutyens and Herbert Baker (who also built in South Africa) reveals attempts to blend Mughal architecture and that of the Italian Renaissance, quite alien to the British homeland. Similarly, the so-called Dutch Colonial style may be colonial, but Dutch it is not. In 18th-century Batavia (Jakarta), the houses were inward looking and sometimes had courtyards and gardens. When the Netherlands government took over Indonesia from its trading company in 1799, it consciously began to adapt local architecture to an image of its homeland.

Both the Dutch and the British began to abandon the neo-classical indigenous amalgam as a model for domestic architecture around the beginning of the 20th century. Although the colonizers built in places remote from those of their own training and traditions, there is a clear connection between these people and ideas, and the Modern Movement in European architecture. There were many probable causes: the nature of the colonizer had changed. While the earlier settlers, often bachelors, usually stayed only long enough to amass a fortune or fulfill a contract, the later ones began to see the colonies as a home away from home and lived there for long periods of time with their families. Other causes were the growing scarcity and value of land and the increasing cost of labour and materials, not to mention the rising expectations of the expatriate settlers and the colonized elite in an industrialized world. Another reason may lie in the idea, particularly after the First World War, that the colonies had to play a role in the modern world, in which case an international architec-

nialen Bauwerken erkennt. In Indien hat man sich entschieden, nicht nur die Macht des Empire, sondern auch die Vermischung des Geschmacks und der Kulturen des Viktorianischen England mit denen seiner Kolonie darzustellen. Der monumentale Baustil der Briten in Indien unter Georg V. während der zwanziger Jahre unseres Jahrhunderts, der durch die imperialen Bauten Neu Delhis von Sir Edwin Lutyens und Herbert Baker (der auch in Südafrika gebaut hat) gekennzeichnet wurde, zeigt, daß man – für das britische Mutterland einigermaßen befremdlich – versucht hat, den Mughal-Baustil mit dem der italienischen Renaissance zu verbinden. Ebenso mag der sogenannte »Holländische Kolonialstil« wohl kolonialistisch sein, aber holländisch ist er gewiß nicht. Im Batavia (Jakarta) des 18. Jahrhunderts hat man die Häuser mit Blick nach innen gebaut, und einige von ihnen besaßen auch Innenhöfe und Gärten. Als die niederländische Regierung Indonesien im Jahre 1799 von ihrer Handelsgesellschaft übernommen hatte, begann sie ganz bewußt, sich in ihrem örtlichen Baustil dem Erscheinungsbild des Mutterlandes anzugleichen.

Zu Beginn des 20. Jahrhunderts gaben sowohl die Holländer als auch die Briten diese Mischung von Neo-Klassizismus und einheimischer Bauweise als Modell für den Häuserbau allmählich auf. Obwohl die Kolonisatoren an Orten bauten, die weit entfernt von denen ihrer eigenen Ausbildung und Tradition lagen, besteht eine deutliche Verbindung zwischen diesen Menschen, ihren Vorstellungen und der modernen Bewegung in der europäischen Architektur. Dafür gibt es vermutlich viele Gründe: die Kolonisatoren waren nicht mehr dieselben. Während die früheren Siedler, häufig Junggesellen, für gewöhnlich nur so lange blieben, bis sie ein Vermögen angehäuft oder ihren Vertrag erfüllt hatten, begannen die später Kommenden die Kolonien als eine zweite Heimat anzusehen und lebten dort über längere Zeit mit ihren Familien. Andere Gründe waren die zunehmende Landverknappung und der steigende Wert des Bodens sowie die wachsenden Kosten für die Arbeitskräfte und Baumaterialien, ganz zu schweigen von den zunehmenden Erwartungen der im Exil lebenden Siedler und der kolonialisierten Elite in einer

pas subi l'influence de l'Europe et de l'Amérique. La colonisation eut pour corollaire la pénétration des institutions locales et régionales, ce qui créa des situations d'affrontement entre les institutions traditionnelles et les nouvelles. Les colonisateurs étaient bien différents tant dans leurs approches que dans leurs objectifs à long et court terme. En outre, les liens entre l'architecture et l'urbanisme des colonisateurs et des colonisés n'étaient pas directs non plus. Ce n'est pas exactement, comme on le croit quelquefois, la domination ou l'imitation de l'architecture du pays colonisateur qui se voit dans les constructions coloniales. En Inde, le dessein des colonisateurs n'était pas seulement de démontrer la puissance de l'empire mais aussi l'alliage des cultures et des goûts de l'Angleterre victorienne et de sa colonie. L'architecture monumentale de l'époque Georges V dans l'Inde des années 20, illustrée par les constructions impériales de Sir Edwin Lutyens et Herbert Baker (qui construisit aussi en Afrique du Sud) à New Delhi, révèle les tentatives de mêler l'architecture moghole à celle de la Renaissance italienne, tout à fait étrangère à l'Angleterre. De même, on peut dire que si l'architecture «coloniale néerlandaise» est coloniale, elle n'a cependant de néerlandais que le nom. Dans la Batavie du XVIIIe siècle (Djakarta), les maisons étaient tournées vers l'intérieur et avaient parfois une cour et un jardin. Lorsqu'en 1799 le gouvernement hollandais succéda à la Compagnie des Indes orientales en Indonésie, il se mit sciemment à adapter l'architecture locale à l'idée qu'il avait de la mère patrie.

Les Hollandais comme les Britanniques commencèrent à abandonner l'amalgame néo-classique indigène comme modèle d'architecture domestique vers le début du XXe siècle. Bien que les colonisateurs aient construit très loin du lieu de leur propre formation et de leurs traditions, il y a un lien évident entre leurs idées et le Mouvement moderne européen. Il y a plusieurs raisons à cela. La première est que le colonisateur avait changé. Si les premiers colons, souvent célibataires, ne restaient en général que le temps de faire fortune ou de remplir un contrat, leurs successeurs se prirent à considérer les colonies comme un nouveau chez-soi et à y vivre avec leurs familles. De plus,

The Institute of Technology (1924), Bandung, Indonesia, by Henri Maclaine Point.

Das Institute of Technology (1924) Bandung, Indonesien, von Henri Mclaine Point.

L'Institute of Technology (1924) de Henri Maclaine Point à Bandung, Indonesie.

tural idiom may have been seen as more appropriate than an indigenous or regional one.

Architecture with a capital "A", seen as a profession with clients, training, international links, and new building types and urban concerns, preoccupied the minority elite after independence. Ideas of Westernization and progress led to new models of development with alternative sets of buildings. However, most building continued on a parallel path – an architecture without architects – based on indigenous traditions, materials, and practises evolved over the centuries. These practises were largely ignored by the new elite classes, although in several instances they were used as a vehicle to illustrate an alternative mode of development by leaders such as Mohandas Gandhi in India (whose focus was more on crafts and self-reliance) and Mao Zedong in China. One can argue, however, that by the early part of the 20th century, urbanization and internationalism had begun to take hold even in countries whose populations were predominantly rural. Concepts of modernization and equity, first focused on urban centres, were influenced by the Russian Revolution of 1917 and subsequent socialist models of development until the 1980s.

Independence, nationalism, and modernity

The practical act of becoming an independent state in whatever form it took, be it a republic, dictatorship, monarchy, or socialist regime, brought with it the need to express a psychological freedom from a colonial or foreign-dominated past, or even from a past seen to be wrapped in the mantle of tradition. This rupture with the symbolic and visual past was first achieved by the Turkish Republic under Kemal Atatürk in the 1920s as it moved to define itself in purely secular terms. It was perhaps the first modern Asian state consciously to seek to express its new identity through architecture in its search for a Turkish identity, as opposed to an Ottoman, ethnic, or regional identity. Turkey succeeded in refashioning itself and became a powerful model for its neighbour, Iran, where Reza Shah moved to build a modern state. The modernization project of Turkey has been a powerful

industrialisierten Welt. Ein weiterer Grund mag – ganz besonders nach dem Ersten Weltkrieg – in der Vorstellung gelegen haben, daß auch die Kolonien in der modernen Welt eine Rolle zu spielen hätten, so daß man von daher eine internationale Architektursprache für angemessener erachtet haben mag als eine einheimische oder regionale.

Architektur wurde großgeschrieben, sie wurde angesehen als eine Berufssparte mit Klienten, mit Ausbildung, mit internationalen Verbindungen, neuen Bauweisen und städtischen Erfordernissen, die die Minderheiten-Elite nach der Unabhängigkeit stark beschäftigte. Vorstellungen von Verwestlichung und Fortschritt sprachen für neue Entwicklungsmodelle mit ganz anderen baulichen Formationen. Der größte Teil der Bautätigkeit lief jedoch parallel dazu weiter, und so entwickelte sich über die Jahrhunderte hinweg eine Architektur ohne Architekten, die auf einheimischen Traditionen, Baumaterialien und Praktiken beruhte. Diese Praktiken wurden von der neuen Eliteschicht weitgehend ignoriert, obgleich sie in manchen Fällen von so führenden Persönlichkeiten wie Mahatma Gandhi in Indien (dem es vor allem um das Handwerk und um Selbstvertrauen ging) und von Mao Tse-tung in China als ein Mittel zur Veranschaulichung einer alternativen Art von Entwicklung benutzt wurden. Man kann jedoch durchaus sagen, daß mit Beginn des 20. Jahrhunderts Urbanisierung und Internationalismus selbst in Ländern mit überwiegend ländlicher Bevölkerung Fuß gefaßt hatten. Die Konzepte von Modernisierung und Gerechtigkeit, die zunächst auf die Stadtzentren beschränkt blieben, wurden von der Russischen Revolution des Jahres 1917 und den daraus entstehenden sozialistischen Entwicklungsmodellen bis in die achtziger Jahre hinein beeinflußt.

Unabhängigkeit, Nationalismus und Moderne

Nachdem der Gründungsakt für einen unabhängigen Staat erfolgt war – und dabei war es ganz gleich, welcher Art dieser Staat sein würde, ob Republik, Diktatur, Monarchie oder ein sozialistisches Regime – mußte man so etwas wie eine psychische Befreiung von der kolonialen und der von fremden Mächten beherrschten Vergangenheit zum Ausdruck bringen, ja man mußte sich selbst von einer

la raréfaction des terres exploitables et l'augmentation de leur valeur ainsi que celle du coût du travail et des matériaux, pour ne rien dire des attentes croissantes des colons expatriés et de l'élite colonisée dans un monde industrialisé, jouèrent un rôle indéniable dans cette évolution. Enfin, une idée importante s'affirma après la Première Guerre mondiale: les colonies devaient assumer un rôle dans le monde moderne. Vu l'objectif, un langage architectural international a pu paraître plus approprié qu'un idiome indigène ou régional.

L'architecture avec un grand A, perçue comme une profession avec des clients, une formation, des liens internationaux, de nouveaux types de construction et des préoccupations urbaines, commença à intéresser les élites nationales après l'indépendance. Avec les idées d'occidentalisation et de progrès, c'étaient de nouveaux modèles de développement qui étaient proposés, et d'autres genres de constructions. Pourtant, la majeure partie de la construction suivit une voie parallèle – une architecture sans architectes – basée sur les traditions, les matériaux et les pratiques autochtones développées au cours des siècles. Ces pratiques étaient largement ignorées des nouvelles élites nationales bien que plusieurs dirigeants politiques du Tiers-Monde s'en fussent servi pour illustrer un mode de développement alternatif; c'est le cas de Mohandas Gandhi en Inde (dont l'objectif était plus centré sur les métiers manuels et l'autonomie) et de Mao Tsé-tung en Chine. On peut cependant affirmer qu'au début du XXe siècle l'urbanisation et l'internationalisme commencèrent à s'imposer même dans des pays essentiellement ruraux. Fortement influencées par la révolution russe de 1917, les notions de modernisation et d'équité, d'abord réservées aux zones urbaines, restèrent des modèles socialistes de développement jusque dans les années 80.

Indépendance, nationalisme et modernité

L'accession à l'indépendance signifiait aussi pour le nouvel Etat république, dictature, monarchie ou régime socialiste –, le besoin d'exprimer la libération psychologique de tout un peuple par rapport à un passé colonial ou dominé par l'étranger, voire un passé recouvert d'une chape de tradi-

model throughout Asia, especially in countries with large Muslim populations, with the success of its forms and its representation of the new state, in ways we have yet to understand fully. Even countries that styled themselves as "Islamic republics", like Pakistan and Malaysia, were conscious of the need to be modern and to be seen as "players" in the development of an international world. In architecture, this was translated into the desire to make modern buildings distinct from those of the past.

Besides the manifestation of "progress" reflected in modernity, the other major trend was that of the social responsibility of the state. The independence struggles may have been spearheaded by an intellectual elite, but they were supported by grass-roots movements. Thus it is not surprising that the model dedicated to equity, the socialist state, was a powerful one that was emulated by many emerging countries, the liberation movements in Indonesia, China, and India being the most prominent examples. Advisors from the Soviet Union played an important role in shaping not only the economic and political face of some countries, but also that of their buildings. Mass housing schemes were modeled on those formed in Russia and, to a lesser extent, on the French public housing schemes. The monumentality of the Chinese buildings of the 1950s and 1960s can be directly linked to Soviet building of the time. The manifestations of the "heroic struggles" can be seen clearly in the statues and monuments to liberation in Jakarta, Beijing, and elsewhere.

States often chose to express their independence by creating new foci for their administrative and symbolic cities, where there was a conscious need to express difference in the new settlements and capitals away from the colonial cities. Although city building was a very expensive process for the state, post-independence saw the emergence of new capitals such as Chandigarh (1950), the provincial capital of Punjab in India, and Islamabad (1961). It is interesting to note that this process also occurred in other Third World countries – Brasilia in Brasil (1957), Abuja in Nigeria (1975), and Dodoma in Tanzania (1976). The capital city or capitol complex (seat of govern-

Vergangenheit noch befreien, die im Mantel der Tradition daherkam. Dieser Bruch mit der symbolischen und sichtbaren Vergangenheit wurde zuerst von der Türkischen Republik unter Kemal Atatürk in den zwanziger Jahren vollzogen, als diese dazu überging, sich in rein weltlichen Begriffen zu definieren. Es war vielleicht der erste moderne asiatische Staat, der sich ganz bewußt bemüht hat, bei der Suche nach einer türkischen Identität seine neue Identität mit Hilfe der Architektur zum Ausdruck zu bringen, um sie von einer ottomanischen, ethnischen oder regionalen Identität abzugrenzen. Dem türkischen Staat gelang dieser Umgestaltungsprozeß, und er wurde so zu einem machtvollen Vorbild für seinen Nachbarstaat, den Iran, in dem Risa Schah Pehlewi begonnen hatte, einen modernen Staat aufzubauen. Das Modernisierungsprojekt der Türkei wurde durch seine erfolgreiche Gestaltung und die neue Art der Repräsentation des Staates in ganz Asien, insbesondere in den Ländern mit einem großen muslimischen Bevölkerungsanteil zu einem starken Vorbild. Selbst die Länder, die sich zu »Islamischen Republiken« erklärt hatten, wie z. B. Pakistan und Malaysia, wußten um die Notwendigkeit, sich modern zu geben und als »Mitspieler« bei der Entwicklung einer internationalen Welt betrachtet zu werden. In der Architektur schlug sich dies in dem Wunsch nieder, sich bei ihren modernen Bauten sichtbar von der Vergangenheit abzugrenzen.

Neben der Manifestierung von Fortschritt, zeigte sich noch ein anderer großer Trend: der einer sozialen Verantwortlichkeit des Staates. Die Kämpfe um die Unabhängigkeit mögen durchaus von einer intellektuellen Elite angeführt worden sein, aber unterstützt wurden sie von den Bewegungen an der Basis. So überrascht es nicht, daß dieses Modell, das die Gerechtigkeit – den sozialistischen Staat – auf seine Fahnen geschrieben hatte, wie ein mächtiges Vorbild wirkte, dem viele der gerade erst entstehenden Länder nacheiferten, wofür die Befreiungsbewegungen in Indonesien, China und Indien wohl die herausragendsten Beispiele sind. Die Berater aus der Sowjetunion spielten nicht nur bei der Gestaltung des ökonomischen und politischen Erscheinungsbildes einiger dieser Länder, sondern auch bei der Gestaltung ihrer Archi-

tions. La rupture avec le passé visuel et symbolique se produit pour la première fois en Turquie dans les années 20 lorsque la nouvelle république turque dirigée par Kemal Atatürk est amenée à se définir en termes séculiers. La Turquie est peut-être le premier Etat moderne d'Asie à avoir sciemment tenté d'exprimer sa nouvelle identité par l'architecture, et ce dans le cadre d'une recherche d'identité purement turque se démarquant de l'identité ottomane, ethnique ou régionale. La Turquie réussit son projet et devint une référence pour Reza Shah, l'empereur d'Iran, qui entreprit de faire de son pays un Etat moderne. La modernisation de la Turquie représenta un grand modèle pour l'ensemble de l'Asie, en particulier dans les pays à populations musulmanes. Même des pays qui s'étaient donné le titre de «républiques islamiques», tels que le Pakistan et la Malaisie, avaient conscience de devoir être modernes et d'être perçus comme des «acteurs» dans le développement d'un monde international. En architecture, ce désir se traduisit par la réalisation de constructions modernes, n'ayant rien à voir avec celles du passé.

L'autre tendance majeure était celle de la responsabilité sociale de l'Etat. Si les luttes d'indépendance ont été menées par l'élite intellectuelle, elles bénéficièrent du soutien de la base. Aussi n'est-il pas surprenant que le modèle prônant l'équité, l'Etat socialiste, ait eu un impact énorme dans les pays en voie de développement. Les conseillers soviétiques jouèrent un rôle important dans l'évolution économique et politique de certains pays, mais aussi dans l'aspect général de leurs constructions. Les grandes cités de logements furent conçues sur le modèle de celles de la Russie, et dans une moindre mesure, sur celles de la France. En Chine, l'architecture monumentale des années 50 et 60 peut être rattachée directement à celle de la Russie de la même époque. Les manifestations des «luttes héroïques» sont visibles immédiatement dans la statuaire et les monuments de la libération, aussi bien à Djakarta qu'à Pékin ou ailleurs.

Les Etats choisirent souvent de manifester leur indépendance en créant de nouvelles cités administratives très symboliques. Il y avait un besoin conscient d'exprimer ses différences sous forme d'habitations et de capitales entiè-

The Capitol Complex (1962–83) in Dhaka, Bangladesh, by Louis Kahn poetically represents independence and the new, modern state.

Der von Louis Kahn gebaute Capitol Complex (1962–83) in Dakka, Bangladesch, verkörpert die Unabhängigkeit und den neuen modernen Staat auf poetische Weise.

Le Capitole (1962–83) construit par Louis Kahn à Dacca, la capitale du Bandaglesh, symbolise avec poésie le nouvel Etat moderne et l'indépendance.

ment) marks the point of transition and signals the change to the modern state where powersharing is expressed through a parliamentary building (as in Dhaka, Kuala Lumpur, Colombo, and Kuwait City), even in instances where the reality of this is illusionary. In fact, Lawrence Vale asserts in his book, *Architecture, Power, and National Identity*: "To a large degree, many post-colonial capitol complexes are, like ancient citadels, a refuge for rulers rather than a vehicle for the sharing of political power. When faced with a monumental parliament building, one cannot help thinking that the line between national pride and governmental security is a fine one indeed." The expression of nationalism, new forms of social organization, and the internal power structure that emerges (usually of the elite) are manifested in urban forms and architecture, among other things.

The state as client has required a new set of buildings to serve as symbols expressing a national and collective identity. (This is separate from earlier symbols, which reflected individual or external power.) These buildings, be they parliament buildings, mosques, courthouses, or other civic structures, are funded and visualized by committees, which usually insist that they project regional, modern, and, in many cases, Islamic references. In trying to reconcile these different imperatives, architects experimented with a multitude of forms, which often led to a curious amalgam of historicist, traditional, indigenous, and internationalist images. An interesting and important example of the expression of nationhood and modernity occurred within many of the states with majority Muslim populations in the guise of the state mosques. The state mosques of Malaysia in Kuala Lumpur (1965), Pakistan in Islamabad (1966), and Kuwait in Kuwait City (1976) testify to the overwhelming desire to express modernity.

It is worth mentioning that the term "modern", as applied to cities and societies, brings with it distinctions of pre-industrial, industrializing, and post-industrial settlements. It is clear, however, as Anthony D. King has pointed out, that these can exist simultaneously today and are not related to time. Perhaps that which distinguishes the "modern" Asian settlement is that it is "usually a

tektur eine wichtige Rolle. Die Planung der großen Wohnungsbauprojekte orientierte sich an den Modellen, die es in Rußland gab und war ferner, wenn auch in geringerem Maße, an den Modellen des öffentlichen Wohnungsbaus in Frankreich ausgerichtet. Das Monumentale der chinesischen Bauwerke der fünfziger und sechziger Jahre läßt sich in einen direkten Zusammenhang mit der sowjetischen Bauweise dieser Zeit bringen. Diese Manifestationen »heroischer Kämpfe« sind in den Statuen und Denkmälern der Befreiung in Jakarta, Peking und andernorts deutlich erkennbar.

Häufig wollten die Staaten ihre Unabhängigkeit durch die Schaffung neuer Schwerpunkte in ihren administrativen und symbolhaften Städten dokumentieren, wo in den neuen Siedlungen und den Hauptstädten, fern ab der Kolonialstädte, notwendigerweise etwas Andersartiges zur Darstellung gebracht wurde. Obwohl der Städtebau für den Staat sehr kostspielig war, entstanden nach der Unabhängigkeit neue Hauptstädte wie z. B. Chandigarh (1950), die Provinzhauptstadt Punjab in Indien und Islamabad (1961). Es ist interessant zu sehen, daß sich dieser Prozeß auch in anderen Ländern der Dritten Welt vollzogen hat – Brasilia in Brasilien (1957) Abuja in Nigeria (1975) und Dodoma in Tansania (1976). Die Hauptstadt oder der Hauptstadtkomplex (Sitz der Regierung) markiert den Zeitpunkt dieses Umbruchs und zeigt den Übergang zum modernen Staat, in dem die Teilung der Macht durch das Parlamentsgebäude symbolisiert wird (wie in Dakka, Kuala Lumpur, Colombo und Kuwait City). In seinem Buch »Architecture, Power, and National Identity« schreibt Lawrence Vale: »Zum großen Teil sind viele der postkolonialen Haupstadtbauten, wie die alten Zitadellen, eher ein Refugium für die Herrscher, denn ein Mittel zur Teilung der politischen Macht. Wenn man vor so einem monumentalen Parlamentsgebäude steht, wird einem zwangsläufig bewußt, daß zwischen dem nationalen Stolz einerseits und der Sicherheit der Regierung andererseits kaum zu unterscheiden ist.«

Der Staat als Auftraggeber forderte neue Bauten – Parlamentsgebäude, Moscheen, Gerichtsgebäude usw. – als Symbole einer neuen nationalen und kollektiven (nicht

rement neuves et situées loin des villes coloniales. Bien
que la construction d'une ville soit une opération budgéti-
vore, la période qui suivit l'indépendance vit la naissance
de nouvelles capitales telles que Chandigârh (1950), pour
l'Etat indien du Punjab, et Islamabad (1961), pour le Pakistan. Il est intéressant de noter que le phénomène se
retrouve dans d'autres pays du Tiers-Monde: Brasilia
(1957) au Brésil, Abuja au Nigéria (1975) et Dodoma en
Tanzanie (1976). La capitale ou le capitole (siège du gouvernement) marque le point de transition et signale le
changement en un Etat moderne où le partage du pouvoir
s'exprime par un édifice parlementaire (ainsi à Dacca,
Kuala Lumpur, Colombo et Koweït), même lorsque ce partage est illusoire. En fait, comme l'affirme Lawrence Vale
dans son ouvrage «Architecture, Power, and National Identity», «dans une large mesure, les sièges gouvernementaux post-coloniaux sont comme les anciennes citadelles,
plus un refuge pour les dirigeants qu'un dispositif de partage du pouvoir. Face à un édifice parlementaire monumental, on ne peut s'empêcher de penser que la frontière
entre l'orgueil national et la sécurité gouvernementale est
ténue». L'expression du nationalisme, les nouvelles
formes d'organisation sociale et la structure du pouvoir
interne qui se crée (généralement celle de l'élite) se mani-
festent aussi dans l'urbanisme et l'architecture.

L'Etat-client exigeait des édifices porteurs de symboles,
expression d'une identité nationale et collective (rien à voir
avec les symboles du passé, reflets du pouvoir individuel
ou extérieur). Ces constructions – parlement, mosquée,
palais de justice ou toute autre institution – étaient exami-
nées par un comité qui tenait généralement à ce qu'elles
projettent des références régionales, modernes, et souvent aussi islamiques. En essayant de concilier tous ces
impératifs, les architectes expérimentaient de nouvelles
formes qui conduisaient souvent à un curieux amalgame
d'images historicistes, traditionnelles, autochtones et
internationalistes. Un exemple remarquable de l'expression de la nation et de la modernité est représenté dans
les pays à population majoritairement musulmane par la
grande mosquée étatique. La mosquée de Kuala Lumpur
en Malaisie (1965), celle d'Islamabad au Pakistan (1966) et

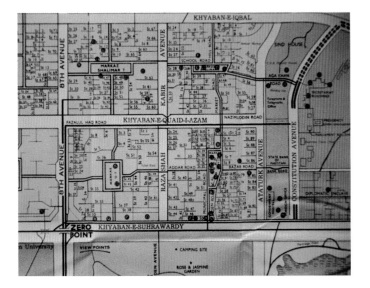

Plan of Islamabad (1961) by Doxiadis Associates
divides the city within a hierarchy of movement
systems.

Der Plan von Islamabad (1961) von Doxiadis Associates zeigt die Unterteilung der Stadt durch Ver-
kehrswege unterschiedlicher Bedeutung.

Plan d'Islamabad par Doxiadis Associates (1961): la
ville s'articule en une série de secteurs et de zones
d'activités rigoureusement.

capitalist city, based on specific energy sources, an
advanced transport and communications system, a complex system of urban government and administration, a
'high technology' built environment, the whole supported
by an advanced form of capitalist industrial city" *(The City
in South Asia)*. Even the non-capitalistic socialist states
aspired in the form and organization of their urban settlements to the same goals, with the exception of means of
control, movement of capital and social relationships –
the physical and technological similarities are striking. For
example, Doxiadis' plan for Islamabad divided the city
into sectors for different groups and income levels, but
provided each with similar public and commercial facilities.
It is not my intention (and it is beyond the scope of this
book) to dwell upon the nature of urban development in
Asia, but I emphasize this as the context within which contemporary Asian architects have had to develop their practises since the 1950s.

Establishing identity and the impact of external forces

The legacy of colonialism weighed heavily on many societies in Asia, even on those only indirectly affected by it.
The role of governmental institutions in promulgating the
expression of a national identity through architecture has
been crucial. However, the influences of Western modernism and of individual foreign architects building in Asia
also had a strong impact.

With the founding of the Republic in 1923, Turkey faced
substantial structural problems, both ideologically and
practically. As the social planner Ilhan Tekeli noted: "The
Republic sought to release itself from the Ottoman image
and to create a national bourgeoisie inculcated with
Republican ideals" *(Modern Turkish Architecture)*. The
eclecticism of Ottoman-Islamic elements combined with
neo-classical Greek and Roman forms gave rise to what
has been termed the "First National Architectural Movement", coinciding with the nationalist political movement.
In the beginning of the 20th century Turkish architects,
such as Kemalettin Bey and Vedat Tek, were trained in
Germany. The influence of modern European architectural
ideas flourished as the Bauhaus and the Modern Move-

mehr individuellen) Identität. Ihr Erscheinungsbild mußte meistens regionale, moderne und oft auch islamische Züge aufweisen. Um diese Vorgaben miteinander in Einklang zu bringen, haben die Architekten mit einer Vielzahl von Formen experimentiert, was häufig zu einem seltsamen Gemisch von historistischen, traditionellen, einheimischen und internationalen Erscheinungsformen geführt hat. In Staaten mit überwiegend muslimischer Bevölkerung sind die staatlichen Moscheen ein wichtiger Ausdruck von Nationalem und Modernem zugleich.

Der Begriff »modern«, wie er für Städte und Gesellschaften verwendet wird, führt fast unweigerlich zu einer Unterscheidung von vor-industriellen, sich im Prozeß der Industrialisierung befindlichen und post-industriellen Siedlungen. Wie Anthony D. King betont, hat sich aber gezeigt, daß sie heute alle gleichzeitig nebeneinander bestehen können und nicht an eine bestimmte Zeit gebunden sind. Was die »moderne« asiatische Siedlung vielleicht tatsächlich ausmacht, ist, daß sie »in der Regel eine kapitalistische Stadt ist, die auf bestimmten Energiequellen, auf einem hochentwickelten Verkehrs- und Kommunikationswesen, einem komplexen System städtischer Regierung und Verwaltung und einer auf 'Hochtechnologien' gestützten Umwelt basiert, und das Ganze wird noch unterstützt durch eine fortgeschrittene Form der kapitalistischen Industriestadt« (»The City in South Asia«). Selbst die nicht kapitalistischen, sozialistischen Staaten strebten in der Form und Organisation ihrer städtischen Siedlungen die gleichen Ziele an, und mit Ausnahme der Kontrollmittel – Kapitalbewegungen und soziale Beziehungen – sind die physischen und technischen Ähnlichkeiten geradezu verblüffend. So wurde in Doxiadis' Plan für Islamabad die Stadt in einzelne Sektoren für die verschiedenen Gruppen und Einkommensverhältnisse aufgeteilt, wobei aber jedem Sektor ähnliche öffentliche und kommerzielle Einrichtungen zur Verfügung gestellt wurden.

Die Entwicklung einer Identität und der Einfluß durch äußere Mächte
Bei der Gründung der Republik im Jahre 1923 sah sich die Türkei mit erheblichen Strukturproblemen ideologischer

de la ville de Koweït (1976) témoignent de ce désir d'exprimer la modernité.

Le terme de «moderne» appliqué à des villes et des sociétés amène à faire la distinction entre habitats pré-industriels, industriels et post-industriels. Il est évident cependant, comme Anthony D. King l'a fait remarquer, que ces habitats peuvent coexister encore de nos jours et ne sont pas liés à une époque. Peut-être la caractéristique de l'habitat asiatique moderne est-elle d'être «généralement une ville capitaliste, fonctionnant sur des sources d'énergie spécifiques, un système de transports et de communication développé, un système complexe d'administration et de gouvernement urbains, un environnement basé sur la «haute technologie», le tout soutenu par une forme avancée de cité industrielle capitaliste» (The City in South Asia). Les Etats socialistes visaient les mêmes objectifs. Les moyens de contrôle, le mouvement des capitaux et les relations sociales sont différents. Mais la forme et l'organisation des habitats urbains présentent des similitudes physiques et technologiques frappantes. Le plan de Doxiadis pour Islamabad, par exemple, divisa la ville en divers secteurs en fonction des groupes et des revenus mais les dota d'installations publiques et commerciales similaires. Il n'est pas dans mon intention (cela dépasserait d'ailleurs les limites de cet ouvrage) de m'étendre sur la nature du développement urbain en Asie, mais je l'ai évoqué pour montrer le contexte dans lequel les architectes asiatiques contemporains ont eu à travailler depuis les années 50.

Le problème de l'identité nationale et l'influence des puissances extérieures
Le legs du colonialisme pesa lourdement sur de nombreuses sociétés asiatiques, même sur celles qui n'avaient jamais été colonisées. Les institutions gouvernementales ont certes joué un rôle décisif en affirmant une identité nationale à travers l'architecture mais l'influence excercée par le modernisme occidental et certains architectes étrangers construisant en Asie fut considérable.

Lors de la fondation de la République en 1923, la Turquie était confrontée à des problèmes structurels impor-

ment found acceptance in Turkey, while four European architects representing the Vienna School – Theodor Post, Ernst Egli, Clemens Holzmeister, and Herman Jansen – came to Turkey in the 1920s and helped to diffuse ideas of modernism, which continued to dominate the country's architecture into the 1940s. Soviet and Italian fascist architecture also had a considerable impact, which reached its zenith in 1943 with the German Architectural Exhibition. Under these influences, Turkish architects turned away from universal approaches toward nationalist ones. This found its parallel in Indonesia where Soviet influence and the nationalist liberation movement in the 1950s promulgated a monumental and nationalist architecture.

The International Style gained dominance after 1952, when Mies van der Rohe and Le Corbusier became particularly influential. By 1960 Turkey had significantly industrialized, a fact that influenced architectural decision-making toward a consumerist mode. As Turkey looked increasingly westward for its intellectual and economic validation, it also began to adopt Western architectural styles, and regionalist tendencies seem to have found only a small voice in Turkey. Although the notion of the progressive, modern secular state resonated well with other newly independent nations, by the 1970s, they seem to have drifted toward examining regional, ethnic, and religious bases for their architectures. In Turkey, there was a backlash in the 1980s and 1990s, with conservative and Islamist circles adding their voices to the development process. Interestingly enough, the intervention of the conservatives within architecture seems only to address the question of Mosque design, which generally emulates the classical 16th-century Ottoman model, while other buildings retain their dominantly international characteristics.

If Turkey is an example of the modern Asian state that had its own empire and had not been dominated by a foreign power, Malaysia, with its multi-ethnic mix of Malays, Chinese, and Indians, poses an interesting counterpoint as a cultural area that was subjected to external influences and a period of colonization and that later styled itself as an Islamic republic. Various cultural influences, notably Chinese, Indian, Portuguese, and the British colonial pres-

und praktischer Natur konfrontiert. Der Sozialwissenschaftler Ilhan Tekeli schrieb dazu: »Die Republik war bemüht, sich ihres ottomanischen Images zu entledigen und eine nationale Bourgeoisie zu schaffen, die eher von republikanischen Idealen geprägt war («Modern Turkish Architecture«). Der Eklektizismus ottomanisch-islamischer Elemente ließ in seiner Verbindung mit den neoklassizistischen griechischen und römischen Formen etwas entstehen, das sich »First National Architectural Movement« nannte und mit der politischen Bewegung des Nationalismus zusammenfiel. Bereits zu Beginn des 20. Jahrhunderts erhielten türkische Architekten, wie beispielsweise Kemalettin Bey und Vedat Tek, ihre Ausbildung in Deutschland. Einen entscheidenden Einfluß auf die Entwicklung der türkischen Architektur übten die Denkansätze des Bauhauses und der Moderne bis in die vierziger Jahre aus, insbesondere als vier Wiener Architekten – Theodor Post, Ernst Egli, Clemens Holzmeister und Herman Jansen – ins Land kamen. Auch die sowjetische und italienische Architektur des Faschismus haben ihre Spuren hinterlassen. Höhepunkt dieser Einflüsse von außen war die Deutsche Architekturausstellung von 1943. In diesem Kontext wandten sich die türkischen Architekten von den universalistischen Ansätzen ab und besannen sich auf nationalistische. Eine ähnliche Entwicklung kennen wir aus Indonesien, wo der sowjetische Einfluß und die nationale Befreiungsbewegung in den fünfziger Jahren zur Entstehung einer monumentalen und nationalistischen Architektur geführt haben.

Nach 1952, als Mies van der Rohe und Le Corbusier an Einfluß gewannen, setzte sich der »International Style« mehr und mehr durch. Bis zum Jahre 1960 war die Industrialisierung in der Türkei erheblich vorangeschritten, was dazu beitrug, daß die Entscheidungsprozesse innerhalb der Architektur sich in eine am Verbraucher orientierte Richtung entwickelten. Als die Türkei sich in ihrem Streben nach intellektueller und wirtschaftlicher Geltung zunehmend am Westen orientierte, begann sie auch, westliche Baustile zu übernehmen, während regionalistische Tendenzen weniger Gehör fanden. Obwohl das Konzept eines fortschrittlichen, modernen weltlichen Staates bei anderen, gerade erst in die Unabhängigkeit entlassenen Natio-

tants, à la fois idéologiques et pratiques. Ainsi que le nota le planificateur social Ilhan Tekeli dans son livre «L'Architecture turque moderne», «la République chercha à se libérer de l'image ottomane et à créer une bourgeoisie nationale imprégnée d'idéaux républicains». L'éclectisme des éléments islamo-ottomans combinés à des formes néo-classiques grecques ou romaines donna naissance à ce qu'on a appelé «le premier mouvement architectural national» qui coïncidait avec le mouvement politique national. Au début du XXe siècle, des architectes turcs comme Kemalettin Bey et Vedat Tek furent formés en Allemagne. L'influence de l'architecture européenne moderne fleurit lorsque les idées du Bauhaus et du Mouvement moderne furent admises en Turquie, tandis que quatre architectes européens représentant l'Ecole viennoise – Theodor Post, Ernst Egli, Clemens Holzmeister et Herman Jansen –, venus en Turquie dans les années 20, contribuèrent à la diffusion des idées modernistes qui dominèrent l'architecture du pays jusque dans les années 40. L'architecture de l'Union Soviétique et de l'Italie fasciste eut également un impact considérable, qui connut son apogée en 1943 avec l'Exposition allemande sur l'architecture. Les architectes turcs abandonnèrent l'approche universelle au profit d'une approche nationale. La démarche turque trouva son pendant en Indonésie où l'influence soviétique et le mouvement de libération nationale des années 50 imposèrent une architecture monumentale et nationaliste.

Le Style International s'imposa après 1952, alors que l'étoile de Mies van der Rohe et de Le Corbusier était à son zénith. Vers 1960, la Turquie s'était industrialisée, un fait décisif expliquant le choix d'un mode consumériste en architecture. La Turquie chercha en Occident ses repères intellectuels, et économiques et architecturaux; les tendances régionales semblent n'avoir eu qu'un faible écho dans ce pays. Bien que l'idée d'Etat séculier, progressiste et moderne trouvât une certaine résonance dans d'autres pays, également indépendants depuis peu, on semble s'être dirigé dans les années 70 vers une étude des traditions régionales, ethniques et religieuses pour élaborer une architecture nationale. En Turquie, un contre-courant se manifesta dans les années 80 et 90 lorsque les cercles

ence from the 18th century onward, played a major role in forming Malaysia's architecture, which was traditionally of timber and thatch. An important event affecting commerce in South and Southeast Asia was the opening of the Suez Canal in 1867, creating a faster and easier route from Europe that facilitated the importation of foreign ideas and materials into the local economies. British imperial connections with India also played their part in the development of the so-called Indian-Saracenic, or Anglo-Indian, styles which were pervasive in the British-designed public buildings of the time. This style took its cue from Indian architecture, exaggerating it with a baroque overlay. Buildings of the 1890s and 1900s, heavily influenced by people like C.E. Spooner, the State Engineer and Director of the Public Works Department (PWD), and the architect A.C. Norman, continued to affect design until World War II. This is not to infer that these were the only influences. While the Malay *kampung*, or village settlements, and the Chinese courtyard houses and urban shop-houses provided alternative models, the British influence was the dominant one. In addition to architecture, the 1933 British town plan for Kuala Lumpur laid down a concept of the "orderly city" (reflecting "civilized" life) for British colonies worldwide. The importance of the PWD in all these countries remains to the present day.

The aftermath of World War II brought with it the functionalism of the Modern Movement and the influence of Art Deco and the Bauhaus. The boxy, wide roofs and projecting slabs used by Le Corbusier, Maxwell Fry, and Jane Drew in India were interpreted by the local British and indigenous architects. Like Indonesia, Malaysian cities also developed their own Art Deco buildings. Also, for the first time, office and government buildings began to use mechanical air-conditioning, as much as a sign of modernity as for climatic control.

British-run architectural firms sprung up in and around Malaysia; Palmer and Turner, first established in Hong Kong and Shanghai in 1882, had offices in Kuala Lumpur and Singapore from 1939 until 1974. Other firms such as Booty, Edwards & Partners (BEP) in Sri Lanka and India, set up offices in Singapore in 1910 and in Kuala Lumpur in

nen durchaus Anklang fand, war sie in den siebziger Jahren offenbar dazu übergegangen, nun das Regionale, Ethnische und Religiöse als Grundlage für ihre Architektur in Betracht zu ziehen. In den achtziger und neunziger Jahren kam es in der Türkei zu einem heftigen Rückschlag, als konservative und islamische Kreise für sich ein Mitspracherecht bei den Entwicklungsprozessen durchsetzten. Interessant ist, daß sich die Intervention der Konservativen in der Architektur ausschließlich auf Fragen der Gestaltung von Moscheen zu beschränken schien, die sich meist an dem klassischen ottomanischen Vorbild des 16. Jahrhunderts orientierten, während andere Bauten ihre größtenteils internationalen Merkmale behielten.

Ist die Türkei ein Beispiel für den modernen asiatischen Staat, der über ein eigenes Reich verfügte und nicht von fremden Mächten beherrscht wurde, so ist Malaysia mit seiner multi-ethnischen Mischung aus Malaien, Chinesen und Indern ein Beispiel eines kulturellen Bereiches, der durch die Kolonialisierung geprägt wurde und sich später die Form einer islamischen Republik gab. Die Präsenz der britischen Kolonialherren seit dem 18. Jahrhundert hat für die Entwicklung der malaysischen Architektur, in der traditionell mit Holz und Reet gearbeitet wurde, eine entscheidende Rolle gespielt. Ein bedeutendes Ereignis, das die Wirtschaft in Süd- und Südostasien tangierte, war die Eröffnung des Suez-Kanals im Jahre 1867, was den Verkehr von Europa aus beschleunigte, vereinfachte und den Import fremder Ideen und Materialien in die heimische Wirtschaft erleichterte. Die Beziehungen des Britischen Empire zu Indien trugen ebenfalls ihren Teil dazu bei, daß sich das sogenannte Indisch-Sarazenische oder auch Anglo-Indische entwickelt hat – beides Stilrichtungen, die bei den von den Briten entworfenen öffentlichen Gebäuden damals weit verbreitet waren. Dieser Stil orientierte sich an der indischen Architektur und steigerte diese noch durch seinen barocken »Anstrich«. Die Bauten der achtziger und neunziger Jahre, die stark von Leuten wie C.E. Spooner, dem staatlichen Ingenieur und Direktor des Public Works Department (PWD) und dem Architekten A.C. Norman beeinflußt waren, übten noch bis zum Zweiten Weltkrieg einen großen Einfluß auf die architektoni-

conservateurs et islamistes ajoutèrent leurs voix au processus de développement. Fait assez intéressant, l'intervention des conservateurs dans le domaine de l'architecture semble ne concerner que les mosquées dont le style architectural imite généralement le modèle ottoman classique du XVIe siècle, tandis que les autres édifices conservent leur caractère international.

Si la Turquie est l'exemple même de l'Etat asiatique moderne, ancien empire jamais dominé par une puissance étrangère, la Malaisie en est le contrepoint intéressant, société multi-ethnique composée de Malais, de Chinois et d'Indiens, aire culturelle soumise à des forces extérieures et à la colonisation et qui se proclama plus tard «république islamique». Les influences chinoises, indiennes, portugaises et la présence britannique à partir du XVIIIe siècle jouèrent un rôle majeur dans l'élaboration de l'architecture malaise utilisant traditionnellement le bois et le chaume. L'ouverture du canal de Suez en 1867 fut capitale pour le commerce de l'Occident avec l'Asie du Sud et du Sud-Est: cette route plus courte et plus facile favorisait l'importation d'idées et de matériaux étrangers dans les économies locales. Les liens de l'empire britannique avec l'Inde jouèrent aussi un rôle dans le développement du style indo-sarrasin ou anglo-indien qui s'était imposé à l'époque dans les édifices publics conçus par des Britanniques. Ce style s'inspirait de l'architecture indienne mais en l'exagérant par un apport d'éléments baroques. Les constructions des années 80 et 90 du siècle dernier, largement influencée, par des gens comme C.E. Spooner, ingénieur en chef de l'Etat et directeur du Ministère des Travaux publics (PWD), et l'architecte A.C. Norman, continuèrent à peser largement sur la conception architecturale jusqu'à la Seconde Guerre mondiale. Il ne faudrait pas en conclure que ce furent les seules influences. Malgré les modèles alternatifs que représentaient les villages malais ou *kampung*, les maisons chinoises avec cour et les maisons-échoppes des villes, l'influence britannique continua de prédominer. Les Britanniques inventèrent en 1933 le concept de «ville ordonnée» (reflétant la vie «civilisée») en élaborant le plan urbain de Kuala Lumpur et l'étendirent à toutes les colonies britanniques. Le rôle qu'a joué le PWD

Art deco style hotel, Bandung; one of the many fine buildings of its kind of Indonesia.

Hotel im Art Deco Stil, Bandung. Gebäude dieser Art finden sich häufig in Indonesien.

Hôtel Art déco, Bandung. Un des nombreux bâtiments de ce style que l'on trouve en Indonésie.

The Social Security Complex (1963–70) in Istanbul, by Sedad Eldem. The rhythm set by the vertical sun shades, cantilevers, and eaves refer to the past within a modern structure.

Der Social Security Complex (1963–70) in Istanbul, erbaut von Sedad Eldem. Die Dynamik der senkrecht verlaufenden Markisen, Konsolen und Dachgesimse nimmt sich in dem modernen Bau wie eine Referenz an die Vergangenheit aus.

Le centre de Sécurité sociale d'Istanbul (1963–70) est l'œuvre de Sedad Eldem. Le rythme créé par les brise-soleil verticaux, les porte-à-faux et les avant-toits constitue une référence au passé dans une structure moderne.

1930. This firm was taken over in Malaysia in 1957 by Francis Bailey and Kington Loo and became a truly local firm. Individuals such as Eric Taylor, who was Kuala Lumpur's Municipal Architect in 1955, opened his own practise in 1964. These illustrations are offered in order to emphasize the continuing cultural influence (as with the Germans and Austrians in Turkey) of British architects in a country struggling for political independence.

Architects in the 1960s and 1970s
Although greatly influenced by external movements in architecture and by foreign architects and training, local professionals began to establish their own, usually individual, architectural agendas. There were a handful of Asian architects practising in the early 1960s whose explorations are of particular interest and importance, coinciding with a period of national consolidation and the search for a modern expression of national identity.

The work of Sedad Eldem (1908–87) of Turkey, the most influential contemporary architect in the country, was modeled on the vernacular residential architecture of Turkey. It was instrumental in creating a recognizably personal style of building and led to the creation of the "Second National Architectural Movement". The Turkish house, with its pitched roofs, solid base, and light, modular timber frame structure, was his point of reference, which he interpreted in reinforced concrete frames and infill materials. The Social Security Complex (1963–70) in Istanbul is a fine example of his regionalist approach that embodies modernist concerns at the same time.

Similarly, Turgut Cansever of Turkey, who has been less prolific than Eldem, has produced work that is more philosophical and intellectually more elaborated. Cansever links function and materials to the context, and uses architectonic layering and its historical relationship to express continuity with the past. His work has been associated with the discussions of regionalism. Another influential practise has been that of the husband and wife team of Behruz and Altug Cinici, designers of the Middle East Technical University Campus (1963) in Ankara. They are prolific designers whose work is sometimes reminiscent of collage,

schen Entwürfe aus. Damit soll nicht behauptet werden, daß dies die einzigen Einflüsse gewesen wären. Obwohl die malaiischen *kampung* oder Dorfsiedlungen, die chinesischen Häuser mit ihren Innenhöfen und die städtischen Ladenhäuser durchaus alternative Vorbilder boten, war doch der britische Einfluß der beherrschende.

Neben der Architektur wurde in dem britischen Stadtplan für Kuala Lumpur von 1933 auch das Konzept der »orderly city« (der wohlgeordneten Stadt) für die britischen Kolonien weltweit (als eine Widerspiegelung des »zivilisierten Lebens«) festgelegt. Das Public Works Department hat in all diesen Ländern bis zum heutigen Tage seine Bedeutung behalten.

In der Zeit nach dem Zweiten Weltkrieg entwickelte sich der Funktionalismus der Moderne; Art Deco und Bauhaus gewannen an Einfluß. Die kastenförmigen, großflächigen Dächer und vorspringenden Scheiben, wie sie Le Corbusier, Maxwell Fry und Jane Drew in Indien verwendeten, wurden von britischen und einheimischen Architekten weiter variiert. Ähnlich wie in Indonesien, entwickelten auch die malaysischen Städte ihre eigenen Art Deco Bauten. In Büro- und Regierungsgebäuden wurden nun auch erstmals mechanisch betriebene Klimaanlagen verwendet, und dies ebenso sehr als Symbol für Modernität wie aus Gründen der Klimaregelung.

Von Briten geleitete Architekturbüros schossen in und um Malaysia wie Pilze aus dem Boden; Palmer und Turner, ursprünglich 1882 in Hongkong und Schanghai gegründet, besaßen in den Jahren 1939 bis 1974 Zweigstellen in Kuala Lumpur und Singapur. Andere Unternehmen wie Booty, Edwards & Partners (BEP) in Sri Lanka und Indien, eröffneten 1910 Büros in Singapur und 1930 in Kuala Lumpur. Diese Firma wurde im Jahre 1957 von Francis Bailey und Kington Loo übernommen und entwickelte sich zu einem echten Lokalunternehmen. So eröffnete Eric Taylor, der 1955 der Stadtarchitekt von Kuala Lumpur war, im Jahre 1964 sein eigenes Büro. Diese Beispiele sollen den beständigen Einfluß (vergleichbar dem der Deutschen und Österreicher in der Türkei) veranschaulichen, den die britischen Architekten in einem Land, das um seine politische Unabhängigkeit kämpfte, ausübten.

dans tous ces pays continue encore à se faire sentir. Le fonctionnalisme du Mouvement moderne, l'Art déco et le Style du Bauhaus s'imposèrent dans les colonies après la Seconde Guerre mondiale. Les larges toits plats en porte-à-faux de Le Corbusier, Maxwell Fry et Jane Drew en Inde furent réinterprétés par les architectes britanniques locaux ou les architectes indigènes. Les villes malaises eurent leurs constructions Art déco, à l'instar de l'Indonésie. De plus, pour la première fois, des bâtiments gouvernementaux furent équipés de l'air conditionné, tant en signe de modernité qu'en raison du climat.

De grandes agences d'architecture britanniques se fondèrent en Malaisie et dans d'autres pays. Celle de Palmer and Turner, d'abord établie à Hong Kong et Shanghaï en 1882, fut représentée à Kuala Lumpur et Singapour de 1939 à 1974. D'autres cabinets tels Booty, Edwards & Partners (BEP) installés au Sri Lanka et en Inde, ouvrirent des bureaux à Singapour en 1910 et à Kuala Lumpur en 1930. Ce dernier cabinet fut repris en 1957 par Francis Bailey and Kington Loo qui en firent ainsi une agence purement malaise. Eric Taylor, qui fut l'architecte en chef de la ville de Kuala Lumpur en 1955, ouvrit son propre cabinet en 1964. Ces quelques exemples montrent l'influence culturelle continue (comme ce fut le cas de l'Allemagne et de l'Autriche en Turquie) des architectes britanniques dans un pays luttant pour son indépendance politique.

Les architectes des années 60 et 70
Bien que très influencés par des mouvements architecturaux extérieurs à la région, par des architectes venus d'ailleurs et par une formation acquise à l'étranger, les professionnels locaux commencèrent à fixer leurs propres programmes architecturaux, généralement individuels. Il y avait très peu d'architectes asiatiques au début des années 60. Leurs recherches, d'une importance et d'un intérêt certains, coïncident avec une période de consolidation nationale et la recherche d'une expression moderne d'identité nationale.

L'œuvre de Sedad Eldem (1908–87), l'architecte contemporain le plus marquant de la Turquie, s'inspira de l'architecture populaire turque. Il en résulta un style de

Page 30: Egyptian architect Hassan Fathy has been very influential amongst today's young architects in Asia and Africa using regional and vernacular models. Illustrated here is a beautiful gouache by Fathy from the 1950s of a villa near Fayoum.
Page 31: Abdel Wahed-El-Wakil, a disciple of Fathy, uses the same vocabulary for the Sulaiman Palace (1981) in Jeddah.

Seite 30: Der ägyptische Architekt Hassan Fathy, der auf regionale und landestypische Bauweisen zurückgreift, hat auf die heutige Generation junger Architekten in Asien und Afrika einen starken Einfluß ausgeübt. Die Abbildung zeigt eine sehr schöne Gouache Fathys von einem Haus bei Fayoum aus den 50er Jahren.
Seite 31: Abdel Wahed El-Wakil, ein Schüler Fathys, gebraucht für den Sulaiman Palace (1981) in Jeddah das gleiche Vokabular.

Page 30: L'architecte égyptien Hassan Fathy a beaucoup influencé les jeunes architectes contemporains d'Asie et d'Afrique qui utilisent des modèles régionaux et vernaculaires. L'illustration ci-dessous est une superbe gouache de Fathy des années 50 qui représente une villa aux environs de Fayoum.
Page 31: Abdel Wahed El-Wakil, un disciple de Fathy, reprend le même vocabulaire dans le Palais Sulaiman (1981) de Djeddah.

borrowing forms and ideas widely from Japan to the USA, and historicizing the Anatolian region's past. Among other designers worth mentioning are Mehmet Konuralp, Cengis Bektas, and the partnership of Dogan Tekeli and Sami Sisa. Perhaps most of the architectural production in Turkey can be characterized as modernist with a passing acknowledgement to the vernacular. It is not surprising that this should be the case given the country's history, the large professional body, and the long tradition of formal architectural education in Turkey.

Another influential country that exported both its architecture and architects is Egypt. Although not in Asia, Egypt has supplied many architects and engineers to the Middle East. In this respect the work of perhaps the most famous and influential architect of the Islamic world, Hassan Fathy (1900–89), has found a wide following amongst younger architects in Asia and elsewhere. Fathy's lifelong efforts to promote indigenous building and the vernacular of the hot, dry climate, provided a counterbalance to the International Style. His poetic use of form, and of vault and dome construction, has been emulated widely by people such as Abdel Wahed El-Wakil (himself an Egyptian) in the latter's houses and mosques in Jeddah, the Development Workshop in Luristan, Iran, Rasem Badran in Jordan, and others in the Middle East.

Two other architects who formulated ideas of expressing an Arab character, giving their modern buildings distinctive identities in the Arab world, are Mohammad Makiya and Rifat Chadirji, both from Iraq. Their use of concrete and its expression of traditional elements, such as arches, in a "modern" manner marked the style of much of the architecture of the Gulf region and Saudi Arabian countries that were experiencing unprecedented rapid growth spurred on by their oil revenues. The desire for rapid modernization in the Arab Gulf states led to the wholesale importation of architecture and technical expertise, often inappropriate to place and culture. It was not until the 1980s that buildings in these countries took into account local climatic and social needs.

Iran was seen in the 1960s as a progressive state, which gave rise to much new building. Large firms such as

Die Architekten der sechziger und siebziger Jahre

Wenn auch unter dem starken Einfluß der von außen kommenden Architekturbewegungen, von auswärtigen Architekten und einer im Ausland erworbenen Ausbildung, begannen die lokalen Angehörigen des Berufsstands ihre eigenen, in der Regel individuellen architektonischen Vorhaben ins Werk zu setzen. Es gab eine kleine Gruppe asiatischer Architekten, die zu Beginn der sechziger Jahre tätig waren und deren Vorstöße von besonderem Interesse und von großer Bedeutung waren. Ihre Arbeit fiel genau in die Zeit der nationalen Konsolidierung und der Suche nach einem modernen Ausdruck für die nationale Identität.

Die Bauten des türkischen Architekten Sedad Eldem (1908–87), dem einflußreichsten zeitgenössischen Architekten des Landes, waren in dem für die Türkei landesüblichen Baustil für Wohnhäuser gehalten. Sein Werk trug zur Entwicklung eines erkennbar persönlichen Baustils bei und führte zu der Entstehung einer »Zweiten nationalen Architekturbewegung«. Das türkische Haus, mit seinen Steildächern, seinem soliden Fundament und seiner leichten, modularen Holzbauweise, bildete für ihn den Ausgangspunkt, von dem aus er diesen Baustil mit Hilfe von Stahlbeton und Füllelementen neu interpretierte. Der Social Security Complex (1963–70) in Istanbul ist ein sehr schönes Beispiel für diesen regionalen Ansatz, der zugleich auch den modernistischen Anliegen Rechnung trägt.

Ganz ähnlich hat auch Turgut Cansever aus der Türkei Bauwerke geschaffen, die in philosophischer und intellektueller Hinsicht noch entwickelter sind. Cansever setzt Funktion und Materialien in Relation zum Kontext und bedient sich architektonischer Überlagerungen und ihrer historischen Bezüge, um eine kontinuierliche Verbindung zur Vergangenheit herzustellen. Seine Werke sind mit den Regionalismus-Debatten in Verbindung gebracht worden. Weitere praktische Arbeiten, die von einschneidender Bedeutung waren, sind die des Teams und Ehepaars Behruz und Altug Cinici, die den Entwurf für den Middle East Technical University Campus in Ankara (1963) gemacht haben. Ihre Arbeiten erinnern zum Teil an Collagen, die weitreichende Anleihen von Japan bis zu den USA machen und die Vergangenheit der anatolischen Region historisie-

construction très personnel et la création du «second mouvement architectural national». La maison turque avec ses toits en pente, sa base solide et sa structure en bois légère et modulaire, constituait sa référence principale qu'il interpréta par une ossature de béton armé et des matériaux de remplissage. Le centre de sécurité sociale d'Istanbul (1964) est un bel exemple de son approche régionale empreinte de préoccupations modernistes.

Turgut Cansever, compatriote d'Eldem mais moins prolifique, a produit un travail plus philosophique et intellectuellement plus élaboré. Cansever relie la fonction et les matériaux au contexte, et utilise la stratification architectonique et son lien historique pour exprimer une continuité avec le passé. Il est associé aux discussions sur le régionalisme. Une autre pratique architecturale intéressante est celle de Behruz et Altug Cinici, qui ont dessiné l'institut universitaire de technologie du Moyen-Orient à Ankara (1963). Ce sont des architectes prolifiques dont l'œuvre rappelle parfois le collage; ils empruntent largement formes et idées aux USA et au Japon, et s'inspirent du passé de l'Anatolie. Citons aussi Mehmet Konuralp, Cengis Bektas et l'association de Dogan Tekeli et de Sami Sisa. Peut-être peut-on caractériser la majeure partie de la production architecturale turque comme moderniste avec une référence fugitive à l'architecture populaire. Ceci n'a rien de surprenant vu l'histoire du pays, le grand nombre de professionnels et la longue tradition de la formation architecturale en Turquie.

Un autre pays important qui exporta son architecture et ses architectes est l'Egypte. Bien que n'étant pas située sur le continent asiatique, l'Egypte a fourni de nombreux architectes et ingénieurs au Moyen-Orient. L'œuvre de Hassan Fathy (1900–89), peut-être l'architecte le plus influent et le plus célèbre du monde islamique, a fait de nombreux émules parmi les jeunes architectes d'Asie et d'ailleurs. Fathy, dont les efforts pour promouvoir l'architecture vernaculaire des climats chauds et secs ne se sont jamais démentis, apporta un contrepoids au Style International. Sa poésie de la forme, de la voûte et du dôme a été beaucoup imitée par des gens comme Abdel Wahed El-Wakil (lui-même Egyptien) dans ses maisons et ses mosquées de Djeddah, dans son «Development Workshop» au

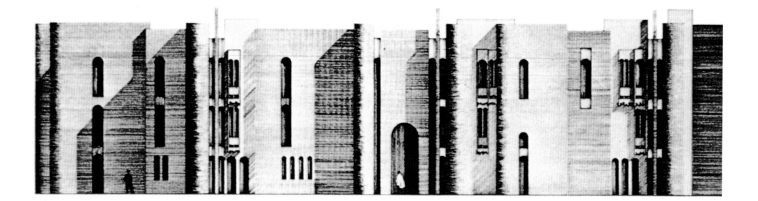

Farman Farmian dominated the marketplace and were a strong influence on the next generation of innovative architects. Two architects who produced fine work were Nadar Ardalan and Kamran Diba, both trained in the USA. Ardalan's interest in geometry and Sufi mystic traditions in Islam tempered his modernist building designs. Diba, also steeped in the Modern Movement, worked almost solely in the public sector and concentrated on housing and community buildings. On at least one occasion they worked together (joined by architect Anthony John Major) to produce the elegant Tehran Museum of Contemporary Art (1967–76), which skillfully exploits the site and creates a complex interplay of internal and external spaces. Both architects have lived and worked outside Iran since the Islamic Revolution of 1979.

In the Indo-Pakistani sub-continent, the Modern Movement had a profound influence well into the 1970s through Le Corbusier, Maxwell Fry and Jane Drew, and Louis Kahn. Most of the architects practising at the time of independence in 1947 had been trained in Europe, but a few, like the doyen of Indian architects, Achyut Kanvinde, were trained in the USA. (Kanvinde went to Harvard while Walter Gropius was there.) The building of the Punjabi capital of Chandigarh brought Le Corbusier to India, where he left behind a number of important Indian architects much influenced by his work. These included Balkrishna Doshi (who completed Le Corbusier's projects in Ahmedabad), Hasmuth Patel, Charles Correa, and Ranjit Sabikhi, to name just a few. Louis Kahn's work in Ahmedabad (1962), and later in Dhaka (then part of Pakistan; now the capital of Bangladesh) where he began work on the Capitol Complex (1963), also provided a model for the region's architecture, championed in Bangladesh by architect Mazharul Islam in his use of brick.

It was not until around 1969, the centenary of Gandhi's birth, that architects such as Raj Rewal and Uttam Jain began to seek inspiration in the traditional architecture of India. In Pakistan, Mehdi Ali Mirza used Frank Lloyd Wright's prairie houses as a model to develop a modern vernacular for his buildings in Sind. However, the modernist and Brutalist tendencies in architecture continued

ren. Weitere erwähnenswerte Designer sind Mehmet Konuralp, Cengis Bektas sowie die Partner Dogan Tekeli und Sami Sisa. Vielleicht ist der größte Teil der architektonischen Werke in der Türkei als modernistisch zu bezeichnen, wobei der ortstypischen Bauweise stets eine flüchtige Referenz erwiesen wird.

Ein weiteres einflußreiches Land, das seine Architektur ebenso wie seine Architekten exportiert hat, ist Ägypten. Obgleich es selbst nicht zu Asien gehört, hat Ägypten viele Architekten und Ingenieure in den Nahen Osten geschickt. So hat das Werk des vielleicht berühmtesten und einflußreichsten Architekten der Islamischen Welt, Hassan Fathy (1900–89), unter den jüngeren Architekten in Asien wie auch andernorts eine große Anhängerschaft gefunden. Fathy, der sein Leben lang bemüht war, den einheimischen und ortstypischen Baustil, der dem heißen und trockenen Klima entsprach, zu fördern, stellte gegenüber dem »International Style« ein Gegengewicht dar. Seine poetische Verwendung von Formen, Gewölben und Kuppelbauten ist von Leuten wie Abdel Wahed El-Wakil (selbst ein Ägypter) in seinen Häusern und Moscheen in Jeddah, in dem Development Workshop in Luristan, Iran, Rasem Badran in Jordanien und anderorts im Nahen Osten aufgegriffen worden.

Zwei andere Architekten, die nach einem typisch arabischen Ausdruck suchten und die ihren modernen Bauwerken eine unverwechselbare Identität gaben, sind Mohammad Makiya und Rifat Chadirji, beide aus dem Irak. Ihre Verwendung von Beton, mit dem sie traditionelle Formen wie z. B. Rundbögen auszudrücken vermochten, kennzeichnet einen Großteil der Architektur in der Golfregion und den Ländern Saudiarabiens, die ein bisher nie dagewesenes, beschleunigtes Wachstum erlebten, das von den Einkünften aus ihren Ölquellen herrührte. Der Wunsch der arabischen Golfstaaten nach einer sich rasch vollziehenden Modernisierung führte zu einem Import (en gros) von Architektur und technischem Know-how, das dem jeweiligen Ort und der dortigen Kultur oft keineswegs angemessen war. Erst in den achtziger Jahren wurden bei den Bauten in diesen Ländern auch die lokalen klimatischen und sozialen Erfordernisse mit berücksichtigt.

Luristan iranien, Rasem Badran en Jordanie et d'autres au
Moyen-Orient.

Deux autres architectes, les Iraquiens Mohammad
Makiya et Rifat Chadirji, ont formulé des idées pour exprimer un caractère arabe et conféré ainsi à leurs constructions modernes une identité qui les distingue dans le
monde arabe. Leur emploi du béton pour exprimer des
éléments traditionnels comme la voûte marqua le style
architectural des pays de la région du Golfe et de l'Arabie
Saoudite qui connaissaient alors une croissance sans précédent stimulée par leurs revenus pétroliers. Voulant se
moderniser très rapidement, les Etats du Golfe importè-
rent en bloc architecture et savoir-faire technique, souvent
inappropriés au lieu et à la culture de la région. Ce n'est
pas avant les années 80 que l'on y commença à tenir
compte des contraintes climatiques et sociales locales.

L'Iran, qui faisait figure d'Etat progressiste dans les
années 60, se dota de nombreuses constructions nouvelles. De grandes agences comme celle de Farman Farmian dominèrent le marché et exercèrent une grande
influence sur une nouvelle génération d'architectes nova-
teurs comme Nadar Ardalan et Kamran Diba, deux architectes de grand talent formés aux USA. L'intérêt d'Ardalan
pour la géométrie et les traditions mystiques du soufisme
islamique tempéraient son architecture moderniste. Diba,
lui aussi imprégné du Mouvement moderne, travailla
presque exclusivement dans le secteur public, limitant son
travail à la construction d'édifices collectifs et de logements. Les deux architectes eurent au moins une fois
l'occasion de travailler ensemble (en collaboration avec un
autre architecte, Anthony John Major) pour produire l'élégant Musée d'Art contemporain de Téhéran (1967–76) qui
exploite adroitement le site et crée une interaction complexe entre les espaces intérieurs et extérieurs. Les deux
architectes vivent et travaillent hors d'Iran depuis la révolution islamique de 1979.

La plupart des architectes exerçant au moment de
l'indépendance en 1947 avaient été formés en Europe,
mais quelques-uns comme le doyen des architectes
indiens, Achyut Kanvinde, avaient étudié aux Etats-Unis
(Kanvinde se trouvait à Harvard à l'époque où Gropius y

The Tehran Museum of Contemporary Art (1976)
by Kamran Diba, with Nadar Ardalan and Anthony
John Major, makes a modern statement with regional overtones in its use of semi-vaulted "light-cat-
chers" modeled on the region's wind catchers.

Das von Kamran Diba in Zusammenarbeit mit
Nadar Ardalan und Anthony John Major errichtete
Museum für zeitgenössische Kunst in Teheran
(1976), stellt mit seiner Verwendung der halb-
gewölbten »Lichtfänger«, die nach Art der Wind-
fänger dieser Region konstruiert sind, eine
moderne Aussage mit regionalen Anklängen dar.

Le Musée d'Art contemporain de Téhéran (1976)
est l'œuvre de Kamran Diba, réalisé en collaboration avec Nadar Ardalan et Anthony John Major.
Cette structure se veut moderne avec des accents
régionaux tels que les brise-lumière en demi-voûte
qui rappellent les brise-vent traditionnels.

This house (1979) in Karachi by Habib Fida Ali, one of Pakistan's prominent architects, is neat and uncompromising in its modernity.

Dieses Haus (1979) in Karachi von Habib Fida Ali, einem der prominentesten Architekten Pakistans, ist in seiner Modernität klar und kompromißlos.

Cette maison (1979) bâtie à Karachi par Habib Fida Ali, un des plus grands architectes du Pakistan, est élégante et d'une modernité intransigeante.

The India International Centre (1962) in Delhi is an early building by Joseph Stein. Laid out between an external and internal court, it has screened *jali* walls that allow air to circulate in the building.

Das India International Centre (1962) in Delhi gehört zu den Frühwerken Joseph Steins. Es liegt zwischen einem äußeren und einem inneren Hof und ist mit *Dschali*-Schirmwänden, kunstvoll »durchbrochenen« Platten, versehen, die für eine ausreichende Belüftung des Gebäudes sorgen.

L'India International Centre (1962), édifié à Delhi, est l'une des premières réalisations de Joseph Stein. Des murs en *jali* disposés entre les cours intérieure et extérieure assurent la circulation de l'air.

into the 1970s with buildings such as Correa's Kanchanjunga apartment tower (designed with Pravina Mehta, 1970–83) in Bombay, Rewal's permanent exhibition buildings in Delhi (1974), Unit 4's Pakistan International Airlines Squash Court Complex (1975), and Habib Fida Ali's own house (1979), both in Karachi. The Californian architect Joseph Allen Stein, who has worked in India for over thirty years, also designed some very fine buildings. These include the offices and guest facilities of the Ford Foundation, UNICEF, and the India International Centre, all of which owe much to the International Style, yet accommodate the cultural and natural context through a well-chosen integration of building forms, landscaping, and materials. Similar in approach to that of Stein's buildings is the Aga Khan University Hospital and Medical School (1972–85) in Karachi by the American firm Payette Associates. The architects' search for a new expression of the desert vernacular of the Sind region, combined with principles of past Islamic architecture and the requirements of a Western hospital building, resulted in a regionally rooted building. It is interesting to note in this instance the role of the client, His Highness The Aga Khan, a major patron of architecture, who demanded a contemporary and culturally appropriate architecture.

As Vikram Bhatt and Peter Scriver noted in their book *After the Masters: Contemporary Indian Architecture*: "Ultimately, it is an abiding faith in the basic Modernist doctrine that underscores the most interesting individual talents of architectural investigation and image-making in India today". This also applies to the majority of architect-designed buildings in much of Asia during this period.

A notable and important exception to the mainstream of Indian architecture is Laurie Baker, who works in South India and whose commitment to affordable building in the Gandhian spirit of service to society has led him over the past thirty years to develop a distinctive architecture in brick masonry, generally using rounded forms. Baker's buildings range from that of small individual houses to larger programmes such as Loyola Chapel and Auditorium (1971) in Sreekarayam, St. John's Cathedral (1973) in Tiru-

The entrance to the Pakistan International Airlines Squash Court Complex (1975) in Karachi by Unit 4 reveals its modern "Brutalist" antecedents within a dynamic building. The spectator gallery is above the entrance.

Der Eingang zum Squashzentrum der Pakistan International Airlines (1975) in Karachi von Unit 4 offenbart die modernen »brutalistischen« Vorbilder des ansonsten dynamischen Baus. Die Zuschauergalerie befindet sich über dem Eingang.

L'entrée du Centre de squash du Pakistan International Airlines (Karachi, 1975) révèle les antécédents «brutalistes» de cette dynamique structure. Une galerie d'observation est aménagée au-dessus.

Der Iran galt in den sechziger Jahren als progressiver Staat, was eine rege Bautätigkeit zur Folge hatte. Große Unternehmen wie Farman Farmian beherrschten den Markt und übten einen starken Einfluß auf die heranwachsende Generation innovativer Architekten aus. Zwei Architekten, die sehr schöne Gebäude schufen, waren Nadar Ardalan und Kamran Diba – beide in den USA ausgebildet. Aufgrund seines Interesses an Geometrie und den mystischen Sufi-Traditionen des Islam fielen Ardalans modernistische Bauentwürfe ein wenig gemäßigter aus. Diba, ebenfalls ein glühender Verfechter der Moderne, arbeitete fast ausschließlich im Öffentlichkeitsbereich und konzentrierte sich auf den Wohnungsbau und auf kommunale Bauten. Bei wenigstens einer Gelegenheit arbeiteten sie (gemeinsam mit dem Architekten Anthony John Major) zusammen, um das elegante Tehran Museum of Contemporary Art (1967–76) zu erbauen, dessen Baugrund sie auf höchst kunstvolle Weise nutzten, so daß ein komplexes Spiel von inneren und äußeren Räumen entstand. Beide Architekten leben und arbeiten seit der Islamischen Revolution im Jahre 1979 außerhalb des Irans.

Auf dem indisch-pakistanischen Subkontinent hatte die Moderne bis weit in die siebziger Jahre durch Le Corbusier, Maxwell Fry und Jane Drew sowie Louis Kahn einen tiefgreifenden Einfluß ausgeübt. Die Mehrzahl der Architekten, die zur Zeit der Unabhängigkeit im Jahre 1947 praktisch tätig waren, waren in Europa ausgebildet worden, und nur einige wenige, wie der Doyen der indischen Architekten, Achyut Kanvinde, hatten in den USA gelernt. (Kanvinde ging nach Harvard als Walter Gropius dort war.) Die Erbauung der Hauptstadt des Punjab, Chandigarh, führte Le Corbusier nach Indien, wo er eine Reihe bedeutender indischer Architekten zurückließ, die von seiner Arbeit beeinflußt waren. Zu diesen gehörten Balkrishna Doshi (der die Projekte Le Corbusiers in Ahmedabad fertigstellte), Hasmuth Patel, Charles Correa sowie Ranjit Sabikhi. Louis Kahns Arbeiten in Ahmedabad (1962) und später in Dakka (das damals zu Pakistan gehörte und jetzt die Hauptstadt von Bangladesch ist), wo er an dem Capitol Complex (1963) zu arbeiten begonnen hatte, waren ebenfalls ein Vorbild für die Architektur dieser Region; und in

enseignait). La construction de Chandigârh, la capitale du Punjab, appela Le Corbusier en Inde où il devait laisser un grand nombre d'émules parmi les architectes indiens: Balkrishna Doshi (qui acheva les projets de Le Corbusier à Ahmedabad), Hasmuth Patel, Charles Correa et Ranjit Sabikhi, pour ne citer que ceux-là. Le travail de Louis Kahn à Ahmedabad (1962) et plus tard à Dacca (alors partie du Pakistan, aujourd'hui capitale du Bangladesh) où il commença à travailler au Capitole (1963), constitua également un modèle pour l'architecture de la région, cautionné au Bangladesh par l'architecte Mazharul Islam dans son utilisation de la brique.

Ce n'est qu'en 1969, année du centenaire de la naissance de Gandhi, que des architectes tels que Raj Rewal et Uttam Jain se mirent à chercher l'inspiration dans l'architecture traditionnelle de l'Inde. Au Pakistan, Mehdi Ali Mirza s'inspira des maisons d'habitation de Frank Lloyd Wright pour élaborer un style moderne pour ses constructions de Sind. Mais les tendances modernistes et «néobrutalistes» continuent à se manifester jusque dans les années 70 avec des réalisations telles que la tour d'habitation Kanchanjunga de Correa (conçue avec Pravina Mehta, 1970–83) à Bombay, l'Exposition permanente de Rewal à Delhi (1974), le centre de squash de la compagnie Pakistan International Airlines (1975) et la maison de Fida Ali (1979), construits tous deux à Karachi. L'architecte californien Joseph Allen Stein, qui travailla en Inde pendant plus de trente ans, dessina lui aussi quelques belles constructions. Elles comprennent les bureaux et les installations pour les hôtes de la fondation Ford, l'UNICEF et le Centre International de l'Inde qui doivent tous au Style International mais qui satisfont au contexte naturel et culturel par une intégration réussie des formes, de l'aménagement paysager et des matériaux. Semblables par leur approche à celle des constructions de Stein, il y a aussi l'hôpital universitaire et l'école de médecine Aga Khan de Karachi conçus par l'agence américaine Payette Associates. La recherche par les architectes d'une nouvelle expression de l'architecture du désert de Sind se combinant avec les principes de l'architecture islamique ancienne et les exigences d'un hôpital moderne aboutit à une construction ancrée dans

Extraordinary Indian architect Laurie Baker produces inexpensive and elegant buildings, such as the Loyola Chapel and Auditorium (1971) in Sreekarayam, on the outskirts of Trivandrum.

Der außergewöhliche indische Architekt Laurie Baker produziert preisgünstige, elegante Bauten, wie die Loyola Chapel and Auditorium (1971) in Sreekarayam, in den Außenbezirken von Trivandrum.

Le remarquable architecte indien Laurie Baker conçoit des édifices élégants et peu coûteux tels que la chapelle et l'auditorium de Loyola (1971) bâtis à Sreekarayam, à la périphérie de Trivandrum.

valla, and the Centre for Development Studies (1975) in Trivandrum.

The spirit of Baker's work and concerns is also embodied in the work of the Sri Lankan architect Geoffrey Bawa, a master of great subtlety and aesthetic appeal. Bawa's buildings remain firmly rooted in the vernacular traditions, so much so that, at times, one feels that they have existed in the landscape for centuries. The prevalent spirit of contemporary building in Sri Lanka clearly owes something to both the international modern and the vernacular-inspired focus on the idea of place. The most interesting buildings stem from the latter not only in Bawa's work, but also in that of Minnette De Silva, Anura Ratnavibushana, and C. Anjalendran.

Perhaps the most eclectic, contradictory, and experimental modern architecture of Asia is in Thailand. In spite of a long tradition of vernacular building and cultural continuity, Thailand has taken both modernity and Westernization to heart since the late 18th century under French and British influences. Bangkok remains both a chaotic and serene city, encompassing change and yet continuing old ways of life and organization. In many instances, Thai architects appear to parody American and European architecture both past and present, and it is here that post-modernism seems to have enjoyed its greatest impact.

In Malaysia, perhaps the first truly local firm, the Malayan Co-Partnership (1960–67), was set up by three British-trained architects who also studied in the USA – William Lim, Chen Voon Fee, and Lim Cheong Keat – all of Chinese descent. Chinese architects dominated the contemporary scene until the 1970s when Malay architects, aided by an affirmative action programme, began to compete more successfully in the country's building boom. Also at that time, new governmental authorities were established, such as the Urban Development Authority, which promoted joint ventures between the public and private sectors. The 1980s saw the profusion of tall office buildings, such as the 35-storey Dayabumi office tower (1984) in Kuala Lumpur by the firms MAA and BEP, large-scale housing projects, shopping malls, and hotels.

The Kandyan Arts Association Cultural Centre (1984) in Sri Lanka by Minette De Silva is built around a curved, multi-purpose stage.

Das Kandyan Arts Association Cultural Centre (1984) in Sri Lanka von Minette De Silva ist um eine geschwungene Mehrzweckbühne herum angelegt.

Le Kandyan Arts Association Cultural Centre (1984), projet réalisé au Sri Lanka par Minette De Silva, est construit autour d'une scène de forme arrondie et multifonctionnelle.

Bangladesch wurden diese Modelle von dem Architekten Mazharul Islam durch die Verwendung von Ziegelsteinen aufgenommen.

Erst im Jahre 1969 etwa, dem hundertsten Geburtstag Gandhis, begannen Architekten wie Raj Rewal und Uttam Jain sich von der traditionellen Architektur Indiens inspirieren zu lassen. In Pakistan nahm Mehdi Ali Mirza die Präriehäuser Frank Lloyd Wrights als Modell zur Entwicklung eines modernen, volkstümlichen Idioms für seine Bauten in Sind. Die modernistischen und brutalistischen Tendenzen innerhalb der Architektur setzten sich jedoch bis in die siebziger Jahre fort, mit Bauwerken wie Correas Kanchanjunga Apartment Tower (entworfen in Zusammenarbeit mit Pravina Mehta, 1970–83) in Bombay, mit Rewals Bauten für Dauerausstellungen in Delhi (1974), dem Unit 4's Pakistan International Airlines Squash Court Complex (1975) und dem eigenen Haus Habib Fida Alis (1979), beide in Karachi. Auch der kalifornische Architekt Joseph Allen Stein, der über dreißig Jahre lang in Indien arbeitete, hat einige ausnehmend schöne Bauten entworfen. Zu diesen gehören die Büros und Gästehäuser der Ford Foundation, UNICEF und das India International Centre. Alle diese Bauten haben dem »International Style« viel zu verdanken und beziehen dennoch den kulturellen und natürlichen Kontext durch eine sorgsam bedachte Integration von Bauformen, Landschaftsgestaltung und Baumaterialien mit ein. Das Aga Khan Universitätsklinikum und die Medizinische Fakultät (Aga Khan University Hospital and Medical School) (1972–85) des amerikanischen Unternehmens Payette Associates in Karachi basiert auf einem, den Steinschen Bauten ähnlichen Ansatz. Aus der Suche der Architekten nach neuen Ausdrucksformen für das Wüstenhafte der Sind-Region und dem Rekurs auf die Prinzipien einer vergangenen islamischen Architektur sowie der Berücksichtigung der Erfordernisse eines Krankenhausbaus westlicher Prägung, entwickelte sich ein im Regionalen verwurzelter Baustil. Der Auftraggeber, Seine Hoheit Aga Khan, forderte eine zeitgemäße und der Kultur entsprechende Architektur.

Wie Vikram Bhatt und Peter Scriver in ihrem Buch »After the Masters: Contemporary Indian Architecture«

les traditions régionales. Ainsi que l'écrivent Vikram Bhatt et Peter Scriver dans «After the Masters: Contemporary Indian Architecture»: «En dernière analyse, c'est une foi constante dans la doctrine moderniste qui marque les talents individuels les plus intéressants de la recherche architecturale et l'image de marque de l'Inde actuelle.» Cela vaut aussi pour la majorité des constructions dessinées par des architectes dans une bonne partie de l'Asie durant cette période.

Une exception notable au courant principal de l'architecture indienne est Laurie Baker, qui travaille en Inde méridionale et dont l'engagement envers une construction d'un prix abordable, tout à fait dans l'esprit gandhien du service à la société, le conduisit dans les trente dernières années à créer une architecture originale en maçonnerie de brique, basée principalement sur des formes rondes. Les constructions de Baker vont de la petite maison individuelle aux grands projets tels la chapelle Loyola et l'auditorium (1971) à Sreekarayam, la cathédrale St. John (1973) à Tiruvalla et le centre d'études du développement (1975) à Trivandrum.

Les préoccupations et l'esprit de l'œuvre de Baker se retrouvent dans les réalisations de Geoffrey Bawa, architecte srilankais d'une subtilité et d'une esthétique extraordinaires. Les constructions de Bawa sont si solidement enracinées dans les traditions populaires qu'elles donnent parfois l'impression de se trouver dans le paysage depuis l'aube des temps. L'esprit qui prédomine dans la construction contemporaine du Sri Lanka emprunte à la fois au modernisme et à l'architecture vernaculaire. Les réalisations les plus intéressantes résultent de ce dernier aspect, et ce non seulement dans le travail de Bawa mais aussi dans celui de Minnette De Silva, d'Anura Ratnavibushana et de C. Anjalendran.

Peut-être l'architecture moderne la plus éclectique, contradictoire et expérimentale d'Asie se trouve-t-elle en Thaïlande. Ce pays a opté avec détermination pour la modernité et l'occidentalisation depuis la fin du XVIIIe siècle, sous l'influence française et britannique. Bangkok continue d'être une ville à la fois paisible et agitée, assimilant le changement mais perpétuant les anciens modèles

The National Museum (1963) in Kuala Lumpur by
Ho Kwong Yew is an early example of expressing a
Malaysian identity using an enlarged traditional
house form.

Das National Museum (1963) in Kuala Lumpur,
erbaut von Ho Kwong Yew, stellt ein frühes Beispiel
für den Ausdruck einer malaysischen Identität dar;
das Bauwerk basiert auf der erweiterten Form des
traditionellen Hauses.

Le Musée national (1963) de Kuala Lumpur conçu
par Ho Kwong Yew est l'une des premières expressions d'une identité malaise prenant pour modèle
la maison traditionnelle agrandie.

While the different Malay states were expressing
their individual identities through their state mosques, a
national identity was being forged in the Federation of
Malaysia's capital city, expressed in its National Mosque
(1965) by Baharuddin Abu Kassim and colleagues of the
Public Works Department. The mosque was designed as
a modern building using a folded concrete plate parasol
roof, which was as much an emblem of the state as a
modern form. The search for an expression of a Malaysian-
Islamic identity was interpreted, by and large, through
the model of the Malay house with its pitched overhanging roofs. The first example of this can be found in
the National Museum (1963) by the Singaporean firm
Ho Kwong Yew and Sons, which, by the 1990s, was seen
as too literal a translation – essentially a scaling up – of the
Malay house. Newer building types, such as the high-rise
building that related to the local context by being respons-
ive to climate and appropriate to the region, were developed later, and were perhaps most successfully explored
by Paul Rudolph in Jakarta and Singapore, and by Ken
Yeang in Kuala Lumpur. The skyscraper continues to be
the most prominent modernist image of progress, as witnessed by the city's Petronas Tower designed by Cesar
Pelli, which, at 450 meters, will be the tallest building in
the world when it is completed.

The situation in Malaysia reflects what the anthropolo-
gist Clifford Geertz has called "nationalism within nationalism" *(Interpretation of Cultures)*. It is found in many Asian
states that were formed by joining or dividing ethnic
groups to create an "artificial" union. The existence of
sub-groups or states has led to some ambiguity in trying to
balance the expression of multiple identities within one
state. It is worth reiterating that the modernist stance was
replaced by the indigenous, largely for ethnic and nationalist reasons.

The city-state of Singapore built commercial projects
and its ambitious and largely successful government housing projects and new towns in a modernist idiom. The
large shopping centre that is now common all over Asia
started in Singapore with the building of the Golden Mile
Shopping Centre (1972) and People's Park (1973) by

schrieben: »Letztlich ist es der unumstößliche Glaube an
die grundlegend modernistische Lehre, der die interessantesten individuellen Talente architektonischer Formsuche
und Image-Produktion im heutigen Indien untermauert.«
Dies trifft in weiten Teilen Asiens auch auf die Mehrheit
der während dieser Zeit von Architekten entworfenen Bauten zu.

Eine wichtige Ausnahme im Mainstream der indischen
Architektur ist Laurie Baker, der in Südindien arbeitet und
mit seinem Engagement für kostensparendes Bauen – im
Sinne des Gandhischen Dienstes an der Gesellschaft – im
Laufe der letzten 30 Jahre eine unverwechselbare Archi-
tektur der Backsteinbauten entwickelt hat, bei der er in der
Regel gerundete Formen verwendet. Die Arbeiten Bakers
umfassen kleine, individuelle Häuser, aber auch umfassen-
dere Projekte wie: Loyola Chapel and Auditorium (1971) in
Sreekarayam, St. John's Cathedral (1973) in Tiruvalla und
das Centre for Development Studies (1975) in Trivandrum.
Dieser Geist der Bakerschen Werke verkörpert sich eben-
falls in den Arbeiten des Architekten Geoffrey Bawa aus
Sri Lanka, eines Meisters großer Subtilität und ästheti-
scher Ausstrahlung. Bawas Bauten bleiben fest in den
Traditionen des Landes verwurzelt, so daß es bisweilen
scheint, als würden sie schon seit Jahrhunderten in der
Landschaft stehen. Der heute in Sri Lanka vorherrschende
Baustil verdankt sich zweifellos sowohl der internationa-
len, modernen, wie der vom Einheimischen inspirierten
Fokussierung auf die Idee des Ortes. Die interessantesten
Bauten kommen von Letzterem her, und zwar nicht nur in
den Arbeiten Bawas, sondern auch in denen von Minnette
De Silva, Anura Ratnavibushana und C. Anjalendran.

Vielleicht findet man die eklektizistischste, widersprüch-
lichste und experimentellste moderne Architektur Asiens
in Thailand. Trotz der langen Tradition seines einheimischen Baustils und seiner kulturellen Kontinuität hat Thailand, unter dem Einfluß der Franzosen und der Briten, seit
Ende des 18. Jahrhunderts die Moderne ebenso wie die
Verwestlichung verinnerlicht. Bangkok ist nach wie vor
eine ebenso chaotische wie gelassene Stadt, in der Veränderung möglich ist, in der aber auch die alten Lebens-
weisen und Organisationsformen weiter fortbestehen.

de vie et d'organisation. Dans bien des cas, les architectes thaï semblent parodier l'architecture américaine et européenne du passé et du présent, et c'est dans ce pays que le post-modernisme paraît avoir eu le plus d'impact.

En Malaisie, la première agence peut-être purement locale, la «Malayan Co-Partnership» (1960–67) fut ouverte par trois architectes formés à l'école britannique puis aux Etats-Unis – William Lim, Chen Voon Fee et Lim Cheong Keat – tous d'origine chinoise. Les Chinois dominèrent l'architecture malaise jusque dans les années 70, puis, grâce aux mesures anti-discriminatoires en faveur des minorités, les architectes malais purent participer avec plus de succès au boom de la construction dans le pays. En même temps, de nouvelles administrations furent créées telles que le Ministère de l'Urbanisme qui favorisa l'association entre entreprises du secteur public et du secteur privé. Les années 80 virent l'édification de nombreux gratte-ciel comme la tour Dayabumi avec ses 35 étages de bureaux (1984) construite à Kuala Lumpur par les entreprises *MAA* et *BEP*, de vastes programmes de construction de logements sociaux, de centres commerciaux et d'hôtels.

Alors que les différents Etats malais exprimaient chacun leur identité à travers leurs mosquées publiques, la Fédération de Malaisie forgea de son côté une identité nationale avec sa grande mosquée (1965) édifiée dans la capitale par Baharuddin Abu Kassim et ses confrères du ministère des Travaux publics. La mosquée est un bâtiment moderne coiffé d'un toit en béton en forme de parasol, forme moderne aussi bien que symbole de l'Etat. La recherche d'une expression de l'identité à la fois malaise et islamique se traduisit dans l'ensemble par le modèle de la maison malaise avec ses toits inclinés en surplomb. Le Musée national (1963) est le premier exemple de cette nouvelle orientation: conçue par l'agence Ho Kwong Yew and Sons de Singapour, cette construction fut considérée dans les années 90 comme une version trop littérale – un simple agrandissement, en fait – de la maison malaise. Des types de constructions plus récents comme la tour, qui parvint à s'adapter à l'environnement et aux contraintes climatiques, furent développés plus tard; ce

The Golden Mile Shopping Centre, or Woh Hup
Complex (1972), in Singapore is a multi-use building
by William Lim, which became a model for much
subsequent development in Asia.

Das in Singapur gelegene Golden Mile Shopping
Centre, der Woh Hup Complex (1972), ist ein von
William Lim errichtetes Mehrzweckgebäude, das
ein Vorbild werden sollte in der weiteren Entwicklung Asiens.

Le centre commercial de Golden Mile ou Woh
Hup Complex (1972) à Singapour est un édifice
polyvalent construit par William Lim et devenu un
modèle pour le développement ultérieur de l'architecture asiatique.

William Lim and Tay Kheng Soon, which were copied
extensively and reinterpreted from India to Taiwan. The
desire to be modern led to the razing of a significant number of old houses, shop-houses, markets, and other buildings, and their replacement by new structures. This did
not cease until the 1980s when the city realized that it was
destroying areas with character and identity in favour of
blandness, and that it was thereby losing touristic appeal
and good building stock that could be revitalized. Like
Hong Kong, Singapore has become the epitome of the
modern Asian city.

Elsewhere in Southeast Asia, Korea has undergone
major upheaval in the 20th century, experiencing Japanese
colonial rule (1910–45) and a war (1950–53) that led to the
division of the country. While North Korea followed the
Soviets in their monumental style of architecture, South
Korea's rapid reconstruction in the 1960s was greatly influenced by European and American ideologies of rational-
ism, functionalism, and internationalism, giving rise to
what was referred to locally as the "simple-structure
style". It soon replaced the country's traditional low-rise
buildings of wood construction with tiled roofs, which had
defined the built environment until then.

The influence of the West can be seen in the works of
the two major Korean architects, the two Kims. Kim Swoo
Geun (1931–86) studied architecture in Tokyo but was
influenced by Le Corbusier, for whom he worked in Paris.
Returning to Korea in 1952, he set up his own practise, the
Space Group of Korea, and in 1960 won his first commis-
sion for the National Assembly. He produced a number of
buildings such as the French Embassy (1961) and the
Olympic Stadium (1977), both in Seoul. An advocate for a
new Korean architecture, he also founded the journal
Space, which continues to be published. The second Kim,
Kim Chung-up (1922–88), also worked for Le Corbusier for
three years and designed over 200 buildings upon his
return from France. Near the end of his career, he turned
toward tradition and craftsmanship for inspiration, as can
be seen in his last work, the Olympic Gate for the 1988
Games.

The nationalist movements of South Asia that began to

The Gumi Arts Complex (1983–90) in Kumi, South Korea, by the Space Group of Kim Swoo Geun, is a major work in concrete with steel trusses and brick facing.

Der Gumi Arts Complex (1983–90) in Kumi, Südkorea, erbaut von der Space Group von Kim Swoo Geun, ist ein bedeutender Betonbau mit Stahlkonstruktion und Backsteinverkleidung.

Le Gumi Arts Complex (1983–90) bâti à Kumi en Corée du Sud par le Space Group de Kim Swoo Geun est une réalisation majeure construite en béton avec armature en acier et revêtement de brique.

Vielfach hat es den Anschein, als parodierten die thailändischen Architekten die amerikanische und europäische Architektur, die vergangene wie die jetzige; und, wie es scheint, hat hier die Postmoderne ihren nachhaltigsten Einfluß ausgeübt.

In Malaysia wurde das vielleicht erste wirkliche Lokalunternehmen, die Malaiische Co-Partnership (1960–67), von drei Architekten mit britischer Ausbildung, die auch in den USA studiert hatten, gegründet: William Lim, Chen Voon Fee und Lim Cheong Keat, alle chinesischer Abstammung. Chinesische Architekten beherrschten die zeitgenössische Szene bis in die siebziger Jahre hinein, als malaiische Architekten, unterstützt durch ein entsprechendes Aktionsprogramm, im Bauboom des Landes allmählich an Wettbewerbsfähigkeit gewannen. Auch wurden zu dieser Zeit neue Regierungsämter ins Leben gerufen, wie beispielsweise das Amt für Städtebau, das Gemeinschaftsunternehmungen des öffentlichen und privaten Bereichs förderte. In den achtziger Jahren gab es einen immensen Zuwachs an hohen Bürogebäuden: z. B. das 35-stöckige Bürohochhaus Dayabumi (1984) in Kuala Lumpur der Unternehmen MAA und BEP, umfangreiche Wohnungsbauprojekte, Einkaufszentren und Hotels.

Während die verschiedenen malaiischen Staaten ihre individuelle Identität mit Hilfe ihrer staatlichen Moscheen symbolisierten, wurde ihre nationale Identität durch den Zusammenschluß in der malaysischen Hauptstadt geschmiedet und fand ihren Ausdruck in der Nationalen Moschee (1965) von Baharuddin Abu Kassim und den Kollegen des Amtes für Öffentliche Bauvorhaben. Die Moschee war als ein modernes Gebäude konzipiert, mit einem Parasoldach aus Faltwerkbeton, ein ebenso staatliches Emblem wie moderne Form. Die Suche nach einer malaysisch-islamischen Identität fand ihren Ausdruck in dem Modell des malaiischen Hauses mit seinen vorspringenden Steildächern. Das erste Beispiel hierfür findet sich im National Museum (1963) von der Gruppe Ho Kwong Yew and Sons aus Singapur, das aber dann Anfang der neunziger Jahre als allzu wörtliche Interpretation – und im Grunde als eine Aufwertung – des malaiischen Hauses verstanden wurde. Die neueren Bauformen, wie etwa die

sont peut-être Paul Rudolph à Djakarta et Singapour et Ken Yeang à Kuala Lumpur qui ont su le mieux explorer toutes leurs virtualités.

La situation en Malaisie reflète ce que l'anthropologue Clifford Geertz a appelé «le nationalisme dans le nationalisme» («Interpretation of Cultures»). De nombreux Etats d'Asie se sont constitués en unissant ou divisant des groupes ethniques pour créer une union «artificielle». L'existence de sous-groupes ou de sous-états est à l'origine d'une certaine ambiguïté dans la tentative d'équilibrer l'expression de multiples identités à l'intérieur d'un même Etat. Il n'est pas inutile de rappeler que la position moderniste fut remplacée par une vision autochtone, en grande partie pour des raisons ethniques et nationalistes.

La cité-Etat de Singapour réalise des projets commerciaux, des programmes de construction de logements sociaux et de nouvelles villes, ambitieux et en général réussis, dans un langage moderniste. Le grand centre commercial que l'on trouve maintenant dans toute l'Asie apparut pour la première fois à Singapour avec le Golden Mile Shopping Centre (1972) et le People's Park (1973) dessinés par William Lim et Tay Kheng Soon. Ces deux centres furent beaucoup copiés et réinterprétés de l'Inde à Taïwan. Le désir d'être moderne entraîna la destruction d'un grand nombre de maisons anciennes, de boutiques, de marchés et d'autres constructions, et leur remplacement par de nouvelles structures. La ville mit fin à cette pratique dans les années 80 lorsqu'on eut pris conscience que des zones riches en caractère et en identité étaient détruites au profit d'une architecture monotone; on se rendit compte aussi que la ville perdait de son attrait touristique et de son patrimoine immobilier qui pouvait être réhabilité. A l'instar de Hong Kong, Singapour est devenue le modèle même de la ville asiatique moderne.

Située dans le Sud-Est asiatique, la Corée a subi des bouleversements majeurs au cours du XXe siècle, que ce soit l'occupation japonaise (1910–45) ou la guerre (1950–53), suivie de la partition du pays. Tandis que la Corée du Nord imitait le style architectural monumental des Soviétiques, la reconstruction rapide de la Corée du Sud fut guidée par les notions occidentales de rationalisme, fonction-

emerge in architecture in the early 1950s did not manifest themselves in South Korea until the early 1970s. Around that time, the oil boom in the Middle East drew construction industry resources away from the country. The end of that boom saw the mushrooming of the South Korean economy and brought major corporations into the forefront as building clients. However, the major buildings, such as the Korean Trade Centre, a Korean-Japanese venture, and the Lucky Gold Star Twin Towers by the Chicago office of Skidmore, Owings & Merrill, were mostly designed by foreign architects. The rate and scale of change may be illustrated by the growth of Seoul itself, which had 2.6 million inhabitants in 1961 and 10 million by 1991. This growth, in conjunction with technologically driven design, led the Japanese architect Masao Shina, who has worked all over Asia, to sum up the commercialisation of architecture in South Korea as "monuments to inorganic functionalism".

The second generation of contemporary architects in South Korea, such as Kim Won, Kim Sok-chol, and Zo Kunyong, were all born in the 1940s and began having an impact on the country's architecture in the 1980s. It is interesting to note that Seoul's designation in 1981 to host the 1988 Summer Olympic Games provided a great impetus for Korean architects to design major projects, including large housing complexes, the Olympic Village, and other facilities associated with the Games. However, the rapid transit system and international airport are being built by foreign firms, while Korean architects, like Singaporean and Hong Kong architects, are looking elsewhere in the region for work, particularly toward China.

Taiwan has not successfully developed a distinctive architecture of its own, even following the restoration of self-rule after Japanese occupation and the Second World War. Architects have been unable to articulate the cultural concerns necessary to project a local identity, as Sri Lankan, Indian, and Malaysian architects have managed to do. Three prominent architects who have been in practise over the years are Wang Da-hung, Han Pao-teh, and C.Y. Lee. Wang Da-hung (a classmate of I.M. Pei) is the doyen gentleman-architect of the old school noted for his design of the Sun Yat Sen Memorial, although he is no longer in

Hochhausbauten, die mit dem lokalen Kontext dadurch korrespondieren, daß sie den klimatischen Bedingungen und der Region angepaßt sind, wurden erst später entwickelt und sind vielleicht am erfolgreichsten von Paul Rudolph in Jakarta und Singapur und von Ken Yeang in Kuala Lumpur praktisch umgesetzt worden. Der Wolkenkratzer ist nach wie vor das auffallendste modernistische Bild für den Fortschritt, was deutlich wird an dem von Cesar Pelli entworfenen Petronas Tower der Stadt, der nach seiner Fertigstellung mit einer Höhe von 450 Metern das größte Gebäude der Welt sein wird.

Die Situation in Malaysia spiegelt etwas, das der Anthropologe Clifford Geertz einen »Nationalismus innerhalb des Nationalismus« genannt hat (»Interpretation of Cultures«). Man findet ihn in vielen asiatischen Staaten, die sich durch die Teilung oder den Zusammenschluß ethnischer Gruppen gebildet haben, um so eine »künstliche Einheit« zu schaffen. Durch die Existenz dieser Untergruppen bzw. Staaten ist es bei dem Versuch, für die vielfältigen Identitäten innerhalb eines Staates einen ausgewogenen Ausdruck zu finden, zu einer gewissen Ambiguität gekommen.

Der Stadtstaat Singapur erbaute seine kommerziellen Projekte, seine ambitionierten und meist erfolgreichen Regierungs-Wohnbauprojekte und neuen Städte in einem modernistischen Idiom. Das große Einkaufszentrum, das es heute überall in Asien gibt, nahm seinen Anfang in Singapur, mit dem Bau des Golden Mile Shopping Centre (1972) und des People's Park (1973) von William Lim und Tay Kheng Soon – Modelle, die von Indien bis Taiwan extensiv kopiert und neu interpretiert wurden. Der Wunsch, sich modern zu geben, führte zum Abriß einer beträchtlichen Anzahl von alten Häusern, Geschäften, Märkten und anderen Gebäuden, die durch Neubauten ersetzt wurden. Dies nahm erst Anfang der achtziger Jahre wieder ein Ende, als der Stadt klar wurde, daß sie Stadtbezirke mit einem ganz eigenen Charakter und einer besonderen Identität zugunsten einer faden Einheitlichkeit zerstörte, wodurch sie sowohl an Attraktion für die Touristen wie auch an wertvoller Bausubstanz verlor, die man hätte sanieren können. Ähnlich wie Hongkong ist auch Singapur zum Inbegriff der modernen asiatischen Stadt geworden.

One of the most modernist architects in South Korea is Zo Kunyong of Kisan Consultants. His 10-storey X-plus building (1992) in Seoul, with a reinforced concrete and steel skeleton structure, stands out in contrast to its neighbours.

Einer der modernistischsten Architekten Südkoreas ist Zo Kunyong, von der Gruppe Kisan Consultants. Sein zehnstöckiges X-Plus-Gebäude (1992) in Seoul, mit seiner Eisenbeton- und Stahlskelettkonstruktion setzt sich von den daneben stehenden Gebäuden deutlich ab.

Zo Kunyong, de l'agence Kisan Consultants, est l'un des architectes les plus modernistes de Corée du Sud. Son bâtiment de dix étages à Séoul construit en béton armé sur une ossature en acier contraste avec les édifices voisins.

nalisme et internationalisme, donnant naissance à ce qu'on a appelé localement le «style de la structure simple», qui remplaça bientôt les constructions traditionnelles – basses, en bois et coiffées d'un toit de tuile – qui avaient défini jusque-là l'environnement architectural du pays.

L'influence occidentale est visible dans les réalisations de deux architectes coréens, les Kim. Kim Swoo Geun (1931–1986) étudia l'architecture à Tokyo puis sous la direction de Le Corbusier à Paris. Revenu en Corée en 1952, il ouvrit son propre bureau, le Space Group of Korea, et reçut sa première commande publique, l'Assemblée nationale. Par la suite, il réalisa un certain nombre de constructions telles que l'ambassade de France (1961) et le stade olympique (1977), édifiés à Séoul. Partisan d'une nouvelle architecture coréenne, il fonda la revue *Space*, qui existe toujours. Le second Kim, Kim Chung-up (1922–1988) travailla lui aussi pour Le Corbusier pendant trois ans et dessina plus de 200 constructions à son retour de France. Vers la fin de sa carrière, il se tourna vers la tradition et l'art, ainsi qu'en témoigne sa dernière création, la Porte olympique des Jeux de 1988.

Les tendances nationalistes, qui avaient commencé à se manifester dans l'architecture de l'Asie méridionale dans les années 50, n'apparurent en Corée qu'au début des années 70. A cette époque, le boom pétrolier au Moyen-Orient draina les ressources de l'industrie du bâtiment hors du pays. Lorsque celui-ci fut achevé, l'économie sud-coréenne connut un essor rapide et les grandes entreprises devinrent les premiers clients de cette industrie. Pourtant, les grandes réalisations – le Korean Trade Tower, réalisé par une équipe coréano-japonaise, et le Lucky Gold Star Twin Towers, un projet de l'agence Skidmore, Owings & Merrill de Chicago, étaient souvent confiées à des architectes étrangers. L'ampleur et la rapidité des changements peuvent se mesurer à la croissance de Séoul, dont le nombre d'habitants passa de 2,6 millions en 1961 à 10 millions en 1991.

Les architectes contemporains de la seconde génération, Kim Won, Kim Sok-chol et Zo Kunyong, sont tous nés dans les années 40 et leur influence a commencé à être

Monumental architecture in the 1970s in the Philippines, exemplified by the National Theatre in Manila by the leading Filipino architect Leandro Locsin, retained a classically modern idiom.

Die monumentale Architektur auf den Philippinen der 70er Jahre, wie sie sich im National Theatre in Manila, das von dem führenden philippinischen Architekten Leandro Locsin erbaut wurde, exemplarisch darstellt, hat sich an das Vokabular der klassischen Moderne gehalten.

Aux Philippines, l'architecture monumentale des années 70, dont le théâtre national de Manille conçu par Leandro Locsin, l'architecte le plus en vue de ce pays, reste d'un modernisme classique et un exemple.

practice. Han Pao-teh, a scholar-architect, was a strong proponent of Western modernism until the 1970s, when he began to shift his concerns to consider the Chinese vernacular in the 1980s. The third and most commercially successful architect in Taiwan is C.Y. Lee, who is noted for his mega-high-rise towers with Chinese motifs that dominate the skyline of Taipei. Today, a younger generation of architects is beginning to emerge and articulate concerns that could change the direction of architecture in Taiwan.

The Chinese in Taipei and Hong Kong responded to market forces, Westernization, and modernization, whereas the Chinese architects in the People's Republic of China came under state control. The "great social experiments" of Mao Zedong and Deng Xiaoping placed priorities elsewhere, leading to uninspired architecture. There are talented architects whose works would have been of interest, had they been able to express themselves or design buildings outside officially approved lines. The same is true for the parts of Central Asia, under Soviet domination until 1991. As for the other nations of Asia such as Syria, Afghanistan, Burma, Vietnam, and North Korea, there is little published, and much remains to be accomplished in terms of scholarship that is accessible to wide audiences. These reasons have made it impossible to locate works of international significance and interest. The Philippines produced some interesting modernist architecture in the 1970s in the works of Leandro Locsin and "Bobby" Manosa, but do not appear to have contributed to the dialogue of Asian architecture in the past decade.

The rapid and uncontrolled growth of the Asian city is well illustrated by Jakarta, which grew from a small port at the time of independence in 1945 to a megalopolis of 7 million by 1990. The country's economic growth through industrialization, its exports in oil and other minerals, the opening of its markets to outside investment (Japanese and others), and a large internal and regional market to sustain it, also brought with it many new buildings and more work than could be handled by the country's architects. Many of the larger urban buildings have been designed by foreign architects from the USA, Japan, Hong Kong, and Singapore. Somewhat surprisingly, local archi-

In einem anderen Teil Südostasiens war Korea im 20. Jahrhundert großen Umwälzungsprozessen unterworfen und hatte unter der Kolonialherrschaft der Japaner (1910–45) und den Auswirkungen eines Krieges (1950–53) zu leiden, der zur Teilung des Landes führte. Während Nordkorea dem monumentalen Baustil der Sowjets folgte, wurde der rasche Wiederaufbau Südkoreas während der sechziger Jahre von den europäischen und amerikanischen Ideologien des Rationalismus, Funktionalismus und Internationalismus beeinflußt, was zur Herausbildung des »schlichten Baustils« (»simple-structure style«) führte. Dieser Stil trat schon bald an die Stelle der traditionellen, landesüblichen flachen Holzbauten mit ihren Ziegeldächern, die die bauliche Umgebung bis dahin bestimmt hatten.

An den Werken der beiden größten koreanischen Architekten, den beiden Kims, läßt sich ablesen, wie stark der Einfluß des Westens war. Kim Swoo Geun (1931–86) studierte Architektur in Tokio, wurde jedoch von Le Corbusier, für den er in Paris arbeitete, beeinflußt. Als er im Jahre 1952 nach Korea zurückkehrte, eröffnete er sein eigenes Büro, die Space Group of Korea, und erhielt 1960 seinen ersten Auftrag für die Nationalversammlung. Er schuf eine Reihe von Bauwerken, beispielsweise die Französische Botschaft (1961) und das Olympiastadion (1977), beide in Seoul. Als Verfechter eines neuen koreanischen Baustils gründete er auch die Zeitschrift »Space«, die noch heute erscheint. Der zweite Kim, Kim Chung-up (1922–88), arbeitete ebenfalls drei Jahre lang für Le Corbusier und schuf nach seiner Rückkehr aus Frankreich die Entwürfe für mehr als 200 Gebäude. Zu Ende seiner Laufbahn ließ er sich von Tradition und Handwerkskunst inspirieren, was an seinem letzten Bauwerk, dem Olympischen Tor für die Spiele im Jahre 1988 deutlich erkennbar ist.

Die nationalistischen Bewegungen Südasiens, die sich in der Architektur in den fünfziger Jahren zu entwickeln begannen, manifestierten sich in Südkorea erst zu Anfang der siebziger Jahre. Es war etwa die Zeit, in der durch den Ölboom im Nahen Osten die Ressourcen der Bauindustrie aus dem Lande abgezogen wurden. Zu Ende dieses Booms erlebte die südkoreanische Wirtschaft einen enor-

sensible dans les années 80. Il faut noter que le choix de Séoul pour organiser les Jeux olympiques d'été de 1988 donna une grande impulsion au travail des architectes sud-coréens qui furent chargés de réaliser les projets les plus importants: de vastes ensembles de logements, le village olympique et d'autres installations liées aux Jeux. En revanche, le métro et l'aéroport international sont construits par des entreprises étrangères alors que les architectes sud-coréens, à l'instar de leurs confrères de Singapour et de Hong Kong, cherchent du travail dans d'autres pays de la région, en particulier en Chine.

Taïwan n'a pas réussi à développer sa propre architecture, même depuis le rétablissement de l'autonomie après l'occupation japonaise et la Seconde Guerre mondiale. Les architectes taïwanais n'ont pas su exprimer des intérêts culturels susceptibles de projeter une identité locale comme l'ont fait avec succès leurs homologues srilankais, indiens ou malais. Wang Da-hung, Han Pao-teh et C.Y. Lee sont les trois noms qui viennent à l'esprit. Wang Da-hung, bien que n'excerçant plus, en est le doyen, un gentleman-architecte de la vieille école, connu pour son mémorial de Sun Yat Sen. Han Pao-teh, un érudit, fut un fervent adepte du modernisme occidental jusqu'au moment où, dans les années 80, il commença à changer la direction de ses recherches et se mit à étudier le vocabulaire architectural chinois. Le troisième, et celui qui a le plus de succès à Taïwan, est C.Y. Lee, connu pour ses tours immenses aux motifs chinois qui dominent Taïpei. Aujourd'hui, une nouvelle génération d'architectes commence à se distinguer et à exprimer des préoccupations qui pourraient changer l'orientation de l'architecture de Taïwan.

Les architectes chinois de Taïpei ou de Hong Kong ont répondu aux forces du marché, à l'occidentalisation et à la modernisation alors que ceux de la République populaire passaient sous contrôle étatique. Les «grandes expériences sociales» de Mao Tsé-tung et de Teng Hsiao-ping voyaient les priorités ailleurs, ce qui produisit une architecture peu inspirée. Les architectes de talent ne manquaient pourtant pas; leurs travaux auraient été intéressants s'ils avaient pu s'exprimer ou dessiner des constructions sans devoir se tenir aux directives officielles. Le même phéno-

tects have played only a small role in developing a new architecture in comparison with Iran or India, for example. With the exception of firms such as Atelier 6 (a loose association of six graduates of the Bandung Institute of Technology) founded in 1969, large firms such as Gubahlaras and Studio T, and individuals such as Han Awal, Gunawan Tjahjono, and Achmad Noe'man, most of them remain obscure. Indonesian architecture tends to follow either the forms of the Javanese vernacular or the International Style. The more interesting work has been for the urban housing assistance schemes – the *kampung* improvement projects – that received worldwide attention in the 1980s for their improvement of the living conditions of the urban poor.

The Asian architects who were most productive from the 1950s through the 1970s were generally influenced by the then-declining International Style, especially by those works of "the masters" that were so widely publicised around the world. At the same time, architects participated in the acts of nation building with optimism, looking for inspiration abroad. Their position was balanced by a conscious allegiance to the emerging states and the need to be seen as part of the modern world that was evident in the West.

Contemporary expressions

In the decades since the 1970s these nationalist concerns and the International Style have largely given way to issues of regionalism and the expression of regional cultural identities. It is evident that the rapid urbanization of Asian cities required new urban patterns and new architectures. The credo of the Modern Movement toward universally applicable solutions broke down in the face of great cultural and economic differences. The attempts in Singapore to meet housing demands followed the functional and need-driven concerns of development without much regard for the specifics of locale. All this changed when the ideas of John Turner (who saw people as a resource and housing as a process), Hassan Fathy (who thought that architect and community should work together in the design and building processes), E.F. Shumacher (whose

men Aufschwung, und die Großunternehmen standen als Auftraggeber im Bauwesen an vorderster Front. Die Entwürfe für die größten Bauten, wie z. B. das Korean Trade Centre, ein koreanisch-japanisches Unternehmen, und die Lucky Gold Star Twin Towers des Chicagoer Büros von Skidmore, Owings & Merrill, stammten jedoch meist von ausländischen Architekten. Mit welcher Geschwindigkeit und in welchem Ausmaß diese Veränderungen vor sich gingen, läßt sich anhand des Wachstums der Stadt Seoul veranschaulichen, die im Jahre 1961 2,6 Millionen Einwohner zählte und 1991 auf zehn Millionen angewachsen war.

Die zweite Generation zeitgenössischer Architekten in Südkorea, so z. B. Kim Won, Kim Sok-chol und Zo Kunyong, war ausnahmslos in den vierziger Jahren geboren und gewann während der achtziger Jahre allmählich Einfluß auf die Architektur des Landes. Es ist interessant, daß 1981 die Wahl Seouls zum Austragungsort für die Olympischen Sommerspiele des Jahres 1988 für die Architekten Koreas ein enormer Ansporn zum Entwurf von Großprojekten darstellte, zu denen groß angelegte Wohnkomplexe, das Olympische Dorf und andere, mit den Spielen in Verbindung stehende Einrichtungen zählten. Das Schnellverkehrssystem und der internationale Flughafen werden heute jedoch von ausländischen Unternehmen gebaut, und die koreanischen Architekten, wie auch ihre Kollegen aus Singapur und Hongkong, sehen sich an anderen Orten der Region nach Arbeitsmöglichkeiten um.

Taiwan ist es nicht gelungen, eine unverwechselbare eigene Architektur zu entwickeln, nicht einmal, nachdem es seine Selbstbestimmung nach der japanischen Okkupation und dem Zweiten Weltkrieg wiedererlangt hatte. Die Architekten waren unfähig, die für die Entwicklung einer lokalen Identität notwendigen kulturellen Anliegen zu artikulieren, was den Architekten in Sri Lanka, Indien und Malaysia durchaus gelungen ist. Drei prominente Architekten, die über die Jahre hinweg tätig waren, sind Wang Da-hung, Han Pao-teh und C.Y. Lee. Wang Da-hung (ein Kommilitone von I.M. Pei), der begnadete Doyen der Architektur alter Schule, wurde bekannt durch seinen Entwurf des Sun Yat Sen Memorial; inzwischen ist er allerdings nicht mehr tätig. Han Pao-teh, ein hoch gebildeter

mène s'est produit dans les régions de l'Asie centrale restées sous domination soviétique jusqu'en 1991. Sur d'autres pays comme la Syrie, l'Afghanistan, la Birmanie, le Vietnam et la Corée du Nord, il existe peu de publications et beaucoup reste à faire pour permettre à un public étranger de s'informer. Il nous a été impossible de savoir s'il s'y trouvait des réalisations architecturales de calibre international. Les Philippines ont produit une architecture moderniste intéressante dans les années 70 due principalement à Leandro Locsin et à «Bobby» Manosa mais ne paraissent pas avoir participé au dialogue de l'architecture asiatique au cours des dernières années.

La croissance rapide et anarchique de la ville asiatique est parfaitement illustrée par Djakarta, mégapole de 7 millions d'habitants en 1990 qui n'était qu'un petit port au moment de l'indépendance. L'essor économique du pays, stimulé par l'industrialisation, l'exportation du pétrole et des matières premières, l'ouverture des marchés aux investisseurs étrangers (japonais ou autres) et un vaste marché intérieur et extérieur, explique l'énorme demande en nouveaux édifices à laquelle les architectes locaux ne pouvaient répondre. Beaucoup de grands projets ont été réalisés par des architectes originaires des Etats-Unis, du Japon, de Hong Kong et de Singapour. Il est surprenant de constater que les architectes locaux ont joué un rôle mineur dans le développement d'une nouvelle architecture, comparé avec l'Iran ou l'Inde, par exemple. Aucun n'a fait parler de lui, excepté l'agence Atelier 6 (une association informelle entre six diplômés de l'Institut de Technologie de Bandung, fondée en 1969), de grandes agences comme Gubahlaras et Studio T et des architectes tels que Han Awal, Gunawan Tjahjono et Achmad Noe'man. L'architecture indonésienne a tendance à suivre soit le style javanais soit le Style International. La réalisation la plus intéressante est le programme d'aide au logement – les projets de modernisation des *Kampung* – qui attira l'attention du monde entier dans les années 80.

Les architectes asiatiques les plus féconds des années 50 à 70 étaient généralement influencés par le Style International, déjà sur le déclin, et en particulier par les réalisations des «maîtres» qui avaient fait l'objet de tant de publi-

Aga Khan Hospital in Karachi (1972–85) by Payette Associates.

Das Aga Khan Hospital in Karachi (1972–85) von Payette Associates.

L'Aga Khan Hospital de Payette Associates à Karachi (1972–85).

credo was "small is beautiful"), and Rifat Chadirji (who called for a new regional modernity) led to a realization that alternative models for physical development were required in regions that needed to face economic and political realities after the euphoria of independence had worn off.

Looking back at this period in the late 1980s, William Curtis wrote: "The international resurgence in the cultural power and confidence of Islam was another major force to influence relationships between industrialized and less industrialized nations in the mid-1970s. This coincided with a period of soul-searching in the west, well reflected in a sort of architectural introversion and mannerism which replaced any serious attempt at expressing human values" (Modern Architecture since 1900). Fueled by the "oil crisis" of 1973, this resurgence began to espouse a kind of pan-Islamism which aimed to express an Islamic identity founded on the unity of the faith, in spite of the different and often divergent histories and realities of the areas of the world in which Muslims formed majority populations. Nevertheless, the architecture of the Islamic states and Asia itself remained dependent on, and subservient to, American and Western European architectural culture, echoing the increasing global homogeneity of building expression.

Very little meaningful alternative discourse (beyond strident proclamations) about architecture occurred in the "industrializing" nations, with the notable exception of the concern for the architecture for Muslim societies instituted through the Aga Khan Award for Architecture in 1977. The Award, the largest architectural prize ($ 500 000) in the world, seeks to examine how built form relates to the needs and aspirations of Muslims living in different societies. The Award served to continue the Western conversations of the 1960s about contextualism and advocacy planning by taking into account regional and local factors, both in the built environment and in social organization. The first set of fifteen awards in 1980 premiated some projects that many architects and critics considered as social processes in building and, as such, non-architectural. This critique was soon overridden by the many who

Architekt, war bis zu den siebziger Jahren ein starker Befürworter der westlichen Moderne, bis er sich in den achtziger Jahren dem traditionellen chinesischen Baustil zuwandte. Der dritte und wirtschaftlich erfolgreichste Architekt in Taiwan ist C.Y. Lee, der für seine riesigen Hochhausbauten mit ihren chinesischen Motiven, die die Skyline von Taipeh beherrschen, bekannt ist. Inzwischen ist eine jüngere Generation von Architekten im Kommen, die sich mit Themen artikuliert, die der Architektur in Taiwan eine neue Richtung geben könnten.

Die Chinesen in Taipeh und Hongkong arbeiteten in Abhängigkeit von den Kräften des Marktes, der Verwestlichung und der Modernisierung; die chinesischen Architekten der Volksrepublik China dagegen waren der staatlichen Kontrolle unterworfen. Bei den großen sozialen Experimenten von Mao Tse-tung und Deng Xiaoping waren die Prioritäten anders gesetzt, was zu einer Architektur ohne Inspiration geführt hat. Es gibt dort Architekten, deren Arbeiten sehr wohl von Interesse gewesen wären, hätte man ihnen die Chance gegeben, sich zu artikulieren oder Entwürfe für Bauten jenseits der offiziell genehmigten Linie zu schaffen. Das Gleiche gilt auch für die Teile Zentralasiens, die bis 1991 unter sowjetischer Herrschaft standen. Zu den übrigen Nationen Asiens, wie z. B. Syrien, Afghanistan, Burma, Vietnam und Nordkorea, gibt es nur wenige Publikationen, und es muß noch eine Menge Forschungsarbeit geleistet werden, damit auch das externe Publikum hier einen Zugang bekommt. Aus all diesen Gründen war es bisher nicht möglich, Werke von internationaler Bedeutung und weltweitem Interesse ausfindig zu machen. Auf den Philippinen wurden während der siebziger Jahre mit den Arbeiten von Leandro Locsin und »Bobby« Manosa einige interessante modernistische Bauten geschaffen; allerdings haben sie zu einer Diskussion innerhalb der asiatischen Architektur im letzten Jahrzehnt offenbar nichts beigetragen. Das rasche und unkontrollierte Wachstum asiatischer Städte wird deutlich am Beispiel von Jakarta, das sich von einem kleinen Hafen, zur Zeit der Unabhängigkeit im Jahre 1945, bis zum Jahre 1990 zu einer Megalopolis von sieben Millionen Menschen entwickelt hat. Das durch die Industrialisierung ausgelöste

cations de par le monde. En même temps, les architectes participaient avec optimisme à la naissance de la nation, cherchant l'inspiration à l'étranger. Leur position était contrebalancée par une allégeance consciente à l'Etat en devenir et le besoin d'être considéré comme partie intégrante du monde moderne, ce qui était une évidence en Occident.

Expressions contemporaines

Depuis les années 70, la démarche nationaliste et le Style International ont cédé la place au régionalisme. Il est évident que l'urbanisation rapide des villes asiatiques imposait la recherche de nouveaux modèles et de nouvelles architectures. Le principe des solutions universellement applicables – credo du Mouvement moderne – achoppa sur les grandes différences culturelles et économiques. A Singapour, on tenta de satisfaire la demande en logements en s'alignant sur l'idée de fonction et de besoin sans se préoccuper vraiment des spécificités locales. Mais les idées de certains architectes comme John Turner (considérant la population comme une ressource et le logement comme un processus), Hassan Fathy (qui pensait que l'architecte et la communauté devaient collaborer dans la phase de conception et de construction), E. F. Shumacher (dont le credo était «est beau ce qui est petit») et Rifat Chadirji (qui voyait la nécessité d'une nouvelle modernité régionale) firent prendre conscience de la nécessité de trouver d'autres modèles de développement matériel pour des régions confrontées aux réalités économiques et politiques après l'euphorie de l'indépendance.

Revenant sur la période de la fin de la décennie 80, William Curtis écrit: «La résurgence sur la scène internationale de l'islam comme puissance culturelle et son affirmation de soi constituèrent une autre force majeure influant sur les relations entre pays industrialisés et moins industrialisés vers le milieu des années 70. Ceci coïncida avec une période d'introspection en Occident, se reflétant dans une sorte d'introversion et de maniérisme qui remplacèrent toute tentative d'exprimer des valeurs humaines» («Modern Architecture since 1900»). Alimenté par la crise du pétrole, ce retour en force de l'islam ne

Institutional Hill apartment building (1988) in
Singapore by Tang Guan Bee is lively and carefully
articulated architecture that maintains a presence in
the urban landscape.

Das Institutional Hill apartment building (1988)
in Singapur, von Tang Guan Bee, ist ein Stück
lebendiger und sorgfältig gegliederter Architektur,
das sich in der Stadtlandschaft behauptet.

L'immeuble d'habitation Institutional Hill (1988)
édifié à Singapour par Tang Guan Bee est une
œuvre architecturale vivante et bien articulée qui ne
manque pas de présence dans le paysage urbain.

welcomed a new way of looking at socially relevant
design. The Award's vigorous examination of architecture
in the field continues to give it legitimacy.

The lack of architectural historians and critics who dealt
with the post-colonial period hampered the formation of a
discourse, as did the absence of international media to
carry it. This changed when the quarterly *Mimar: Architecture in Development*, came into being (1981–92). It was
the only international Asian-based journal to examine architecture in relation to culture, and to promote cross-cultural
exchange and the presentation of pluralistic viewpoints.
Similar in purpose to the Aga Khan Award for Architecture,
but different in that it included unbuilt projects and theor-
etical writings, it did not limit itself to Muslim societies but
published works from all over the Third World.

A number of individuals, besides Hassan Fathy and
Sedad Eldem, began to articulate their concerns about
contemporary architecture in published works, but they
remained on the fringe of their own societies in terms of
intellectual exchange. In Southeast Asia, a small group of
architects trained in the West formed APAC (Asian Planning and Architectural Collaboration) to look at issues of
national and Asian identity, and issues related to professional practise. This group consisted of Fuhimiko Maki and
Koichi Nagashima of Japan, Tao Ho of Hong Kong, William
Lim of Singapore, Sumet Jumsai of Thailand, and Charles
Correa of India, all of whom became important figures by
the 1980s. These and other Asian theoreticians, architects,
and historians often framed their ideas within the discourse established by influential critics from the West.

In the late 1970s and 1980s, some architects in Asia
began to reconsider the „skin-deep modernism and
glib traditionalism" (to use William Curtis' phrase). The
attempt to produce a synthesis was made by both indigenous and foreign architects in a wide variety of ways that
reflected personal, regional, and international concerns. It
had become impossible to be totally local, and contextual
aspects had to be considered alongside questions of
globalization. By the 1980s, even mainstream architects
like Paul Rudolph, Kenzo Tange, I.M. Pei, and Foster Associates, to name just a few, attempted to produce architec-

The citadel-like Ministry of Foreign Affairs (1984) in Riyadh by Danish architect Henning Larsen displays an understanding of site, climate, and culture. The project won an Aga Khan Award for Architecture in 1989.

Das von dem dänischen Architekten Henning Larsen in Form einer Zitadelle erbaute Außenministerium (1984) in Riyadh läßt eine Vertrautheit mit dem Ort, dem Klima und der Kultur erkennen. Das Projekt wurde 1989 mit dem Aga Khan Award for Architecture ausgezeichnet.

Œuvre de l'architecte danois Henning Larsen, le Ministère des Affaires étrangères de Riyad (1984), qui a l'apparence d'une citadelle, met en harmonie le site, le climat et la culture. Ce projet a reçu l'Aga Khan Award for Architecture en 1989.

Wirtschaftswachstum des Landes, seine Exporte von Öl und anderen Bodenschätzen, die Öffnung seiner Märkte gegenüber Investitionen aus dem Ausland (aus Japan und anderen Staaten) sowie der große Binnen- und Regionalmarkt zur Unterstützung all dessen, hatte zur Folge, daß viele Neubauten errichtet wurden und es mehr Arbeit gab, als die Architekten des Landes bewältigen konnten. Viele der größeren städtischen Bauten sind von ausländischen Architekten aus den USA, Japan, Hongkong und Singapur entworfen worden. Es überrascht ein wenig, daß die ortsansässigen Architekten eine so geringe Rolle bei der Entwicklung der Architektur gespielt haben, verglichen z. B. mit deren Rolle im Iran oder in Indien. Mit Ausnahme solcher Gruppen wie dem Atelier 6 (einem losen Zusammenschluß von sechs Absolventen des Bandung Institute of Technology), das 1969 gegründet wurde, großer Unternehmen wie Gubahlaras und Studio T und einzelner Architekten wie Han Awal, Gunawan Tjahjono und Achmad Noe'man, bleiben die meisten von ihnen unbekannt. Tendenziell orientiert sich die indonesische Architektur entweder an dem typisch javanischen Baustil oder aber am »International Style«. Die interessanteren Arbeiten entstanden im Zusammenhang mit den Hilfsprogrammen für den städtischen Wohnungsbau – den *Kampung* Sanierungsprojekten – die in den Achtzigern wegen ihres Beitrags zur Verbesserung der Lebensbedingungen der armen Stadtbevölkerung weltweite Beachtung fanden.

Zeitgenössische Ausdrucksformen

Seit den achtziger Jahren waren die nationalistischen Anliegen und der »International Style« bereits weitgehend den Problemen des Regionalismus und der Notwendigkeit des Ausdrucks einer regionalen kulturellen Identität gewichen. Offensichtlich machte die sich rasch entwickelnde Urbanisierung der asiatischen Städte neue Stadtstrukturen und neue Formen der Architektur erforderlich. Das Credo der Moderne, das sich an universell verwendbaren Lösungen orientierte, brach in Anbetracht der starken kulturellen und ökonomischen Differenzen zusammen. Die Versuche, die in Singapur zur Deckung des Wohnungsbedarfs gemacht wurden, folgten den funktionalen und von der Not

tarda pas à se rattacher à une sorte de panislamisme. Soucieux d'exprimer une identité islamique fondée sur l'unité de la foi et non sur des réalités et des passés différents – et souvent divergents – des régions du monde où les musulmans constituaient la majorité de la population. Reste que l'architecture des Etats musulmans et l'Asie continuaient à s'aligner sur la culture architecturale américaine et européenne, faisant ainsi écho à la mondialisation de l'expression architecturale.

Dans les nations en «voie d'industrialisation», il n'y eut guère de discours architectural proposant une alternative sérieuse (au-delà des déclarations tonitruantes). Cependant, l'exception qui confirme la règle est le prix d'architecture créé en 1977 par l'Aga Khan, qui montrait ainsi son intérêt pour l'architecture adaptée aux sociétés musulmanes. Le prix, le plus important au monde dans le domaine de l'architecture (montant: 500 000 $), souhaite encourager la recherche de formes bâties correspondant aux besoins et aux aspirations de musulmans vivant dans différentes sociétés. Il se veut le prolongement de la discussion qui eut cours en Occident dans les années 60 sur la question du contexte et du plan au service d'une fonction en tenant compte des facteurs régionaux et locaux, à la fois dans l'environnement bâti et dans l'organisation sociale. Les premiers quinze prix attribués en 1980 récompensaient certains projets que de nombreux architectes et critiques considérèrent comme de simples gestes sociaux qui n'avaient rien d'architectural. Cette critique fut vite battue en brèche par ceux nombreux, qui firent bon accueil à cette nouvelle manière d'envisager l'architecture «sociale». C'est parce qu'il juge l'architecture sur le terrain que le Prix Aga Khan reste pertinent.

L'absence d'historiens et de critiques de l'architecture post-coloniale entravait l'élaboration d'un discours architectural, tout comme le manque d'accès aux médias internationaux. Mais la parution de la revue trimestrielle «Mimar: Architecture in Development» (1981–92) changea les choses. C'était alors la seule publication asiatique à vocation internationale à étudier l'architecture par rapport à la culture, à promouvoir un échange multiculturel et à présenter une pluralité de points de vue. Comparable au

ture that responded to place, time, culture, and local aspirations. This is generally not true of their earlier work in Asia.

Some architects like Habib Fida Ali, Won Kim and Tao Ho, remained rooted in modernism. Others, like William Lim and Sumet Jumsai, embraced the post-modern and deconstructivist views of architecture. Simultaneously, Geoffrey Bawa, Laurie Baker, and Jimmy Lim continued to work interpreting the vernacular while the work of Rasem Badran and others adopted a historicist approach recalling the high achievements of past cultures before the advent of Western colonialism. Others, such as Nira Gandhi in India and Tang Guan Bee in Singapore, have produced interesting and eclectic new work.

In summary: since the 1950s two major phases of architectural production can be identified. The first introduced modernism and the International Style, which arrived with a flourish and remained a force, declining only in the 1980s. The second embraced versions of regionalism, transforming the vernacular and referring to history to address emerging concerns about identity. This phase gained momentum in the early 1980s, although it existed earlier. Since the mid-1980s, almost as a reflection of the profusion of information and images transmitted globally, architecture in Asia has produced a wide range of eclectic expressions in which stylistic directions are indiscernible.

Cities in Asia are growing at an unprecedented rate. By the year 2000, some fifteen of the world's twenty most populous cities will be Asian, and people of different ethnic, religious, and social backgrounds will live in them. The range of new technology and methods of exchange, multinational organizations and concerns, allow for the management and diffusion of pluralistic expressions in architecture. These aspects of multi-culturalism are already a reality, and strikingly evident in many regions of Asia, which is well situated to deal with these new realities and changing world order of the 21st century. The upheavals in the Central Asian republics, the emergence of South and East Asian states as world players, and the international economic and political force of China, are affecting worldwide events and relationships, and, consequently, Asian architecture itself.

diktierten baulichen Erfordernissen, und lokale Besonderheiten fanden dabei wenig Berücksichtigung. All das änderte sich, als die Ideen John Turners (der die Menschen als Resourcen und den Wohnungsbau als Prozeß begriff), Hassan Fathys (der der Ansicht war, daß Architekten und Kommunen bei den Prozessen des Entwerfens und Bauens zusammenarbeiten sollten), E.F. Shumachers (dessen Credo lautete: »small is beautiful«) und Rifat Chadirjis (der eine neue regionale Modernität forderte), zu der Einsicht führten, daß man alternative Modelle zur physischen Entwicklung von Regionen brauchte, die sich nun den ökonomischen und politischen Realitäten zu stellen hatten, nachdem sich die Euphorie der Unabhängigkeit gelegt hatte.

Im Rückblick auf das Ende der achtziger Jahre schrieb William Curtis: »Das internationale Wiederaufleben der kulturellen Macht und des Vertrauens in den Islam stellte eine weitere bedeutende Kraft dar, die die Beziehungen zwischen den industrialisierten und den weniger industrialisierten Nationen Mitte der siebziger Jahre beeinflußte. Dies fiel im Westen mit einer Zeit der Sinnsuche zusammen, die sich in einer Art architektonischer Introvertiertheit und einem Manierismus widerspiegelte, der an die Stelle jedes ernst zu nehmenden Versuches trat, für menschliche Werte eine Ausdrucksmöglichkeit zu finden« (»Modern Architecture since 1900«). Ausgelöst durch die »Ölkrise« im Jahre 1973, verband sich dieses Wiederaufleben allmählich mit einer Art Pan-Islamismus, dem es darum ging, für eine sich auf die Einheit des Glaubens gründende islamische Identität einen Ausdruck zu finden. Trotzdem blieb die Architektur der islamischen Staaten und Asiens abhängig von (und unterwürfig gegenüber) der amerikanischen und westeuropäischen Architektur und spiegelte so die weltweit zunehmende Homogenität des baulichen Ausdrucks.

Bei den Nationen, die sich im Prozeß der Industrialisierung befanden, gab es kaum bedeutsame alternative Diskurse über Architektur (die über glühende Proklamationen hinausgegangen wären), mit Ausnahme eines in der Tat bemerkenswerten Eintretens für die Architektur muslimischer Gesellschaften, das durch den Aga Khan Award for Architecture im Jahre 1977 institutionalisiert wurde. Mit-

Prix Aga Khan par son objet mais publiant aussi des projets non réalisés et des articles théoriques, ne se limitait pas aux sociétés musulmanes et informait sur toute l'architecture du Tiers-Monde.

Certains architectes, en dehors de Hassan Fathy et de Sedad Eldem, commencèrent à exprimer leurs idées en matière d'architecture contemporaine dans diverses publications et livres, mais ils restaient en marge de la vie intellectuelle de leur pays: dans le Sud-Est asiatique, un petit groupe d'architectes formés en Occident créèrent l'APAC (Asian Planning, and Architectural Collaboration) pour se pencher sur les questions de pratique architecturale et d'identité nationale et asiatique. Les membres de ce groupe – Fuhimiko Maki et Koichi Nagashima du Japon, Tao Ho de Hong Kong, William Lim de Singapour, Sumet Jumsai de Thaïlande et Charles Correa d'Inde – deviendront tous des personnalités de l'architecture dans les années 80. Eux et d'autres théoriciens asiatiques, des architectes et des historiens formulèrent souvent leurs idées dans le cadre du discours établi par des critiques occidentaux influents.

Vers le milieu des années 70 et 80, des architectes d'Asie se mirent à reconsidérer le «modernisme superficiel et le traditionalisme désinvolte» (pour reprendre les termes de William Curtis). La recherche de cette synthèse était menée par des architectes autochtones et étrangers selon des formules très variées reflétant les préoccupations personnelles, régionales et internationales. Etre entièrement local étant devenu impossible, les aspects contextuels durent être considérés parallèlement aux questions de mondialisation. Au cours de la décennie 80, même des architectes influents comme Paul Rudolph, Kenzo Tange, I.M. Pei ou Foster Associates, cherchèrent à créer une architecture adaptée au lieu, à la culture et aux aspirations locales. On ne peut en dire autant de leurs premières réalisations en Asie.

Certains architectes tels Habib Fida Ali, Won Kim et Tao Ho restaient ancrés dans le modernisme. Les réalisations d'autres architectes comme William Lim et Sumet Jumsai se référaient au post-modernisme et au déconstructivisme. Dans le même temps, Geoffrey Bawa, Laurie Baker

An eccentric and pleasing holiday house (1992) in Maharastra, southern India, by Nira Gandhi combines elements and styles to produce a deconstructivist hybrid architecture.

Das ebenso ausgefallene wie ansprechende Ferienhaus (1992) in Maharastra, Südindien, von Nira Gandhi, vereint verschiedene Elemente und Stilrichtungen zu einer dekonstruktivistischen Mischarchitektur.

Cette résidence de vacances agréable et originale, réalisée par Nira Gandhi, à Maharastra (1992) dans le sud de l'Inde, fusionne divers éléments et styles en une architecture hybride déconstructiviste.

Asian cities are changing rapidly. The character of cities like Istanbul (depicted in the cartoon) may be lost in the anonymous towers of the 20th century; but technology may help humanize them to produce, as proclaimed on a t-shirt in Singapore, "a great place to live".

Asiens Städte sind einer raschen Veränderung unterworfen. Der spezifische Charakter solcher Städte wie Istanbul (in der Karikatur dargestellt) mag in der Anonymität der Wohntürme des 20. Jahrhunderts verloren gehen; aber die Technik ermöglicht vielleicht eine menschengerechtere Gestaltung.

Les cités asiatiques se transforment rapidement. Des villes comme Istanbul (représentée sur le dessin) risquent de perdre leur caractère propre dans l'anonymat des tours du XXe siècle. Pourtant, la technologie peut permettre de les humaniser.

hilfe dieses Preises, dem größten Architektur-Preis ($ 500 000) der Welt, soll untersucht werden, in welcher Beziehung die baulichen Formen zu den Bedürfnissen und Wünschen der Muslime stehen, die in den verschiedenen Gesellschaften leben. Dieser Preis hat dazu beigetragen, daß die im Westen während der sechziger Jahre geführten Diskussionen über Kontextualität und beratende Planung in dem Sinne fortgesetzt wurden, daß auch regionale und lokale Faktoren berücksichtigt wurden, sowohl was die bauliche Umgebung als auch die soziale Organisation angeht. Mit den ersten 15, im Jahre 1980 vergebenen Preisen wurde eine Reihe von Projekten ausgezeichnet, die von vielen Architekten und Kritikern eher als gesellschaftliche Prozesse im Bauwesen angesehen wurden und die für sie folglich keine echten architektonischen Projekte darstellten. Diese Kritik wurde aber bald verworfen, da viele eine neue Sichtweise der gesellschaftlich relevanten Entwürfe begrüßten.

Die Tatsache, daß es so wenige Architektur-Historiker und Kritiker gab, die sich mit der postkolonialen Zeit befaßten, wirkte sich auf die Entstehung eines Diskurses ebenso hemmend aus, wie das Fehlen von internationalen Medien auf dessen Verbreitung. Das änderte sich, als die Vierteljahresschrift »Mimar: Architecture in Development« ins Leben gerufen wurde (1981–92). Es war die einzige internationale, in Asien erscheinende Zeitschrift, die die Architektur in ihrem Verhältnis zur Kultur untersuchte und für einen kulturellen Austausch und die Bekanntmachung eines pluralistischen Denkens eintrat. Diese Zeitschrift war ähnlich konzipiert wie der Aga-Khan-Preis für Architektur, aber sie befaßte sich auch mit nicht gebauten Projekten und theoretischen Schriften und veröffentlichte Berichte über Arbeiten aus allen Ländern der Dritten Welt.

Einzelne begannen dann, neben Hassan Fathy und Sedad Eldem, das, worauf es ihnen in der modernen Architektur ankam, zu veröffentlichen. Was den intellektuellen Austausch anbelangt, blieben sie allerdings selbst innerhalb ihrer eigenen Gesellschaften nur Randfiguren. In Südostasien gründete eine kleine Gruppe von im Westen ausgebildeten Architekten die APAC (Asian Planning and Architectural Collaboration), um sich mit Fragen der natio-

et Jimmy Lim continuaient à interpréter l'architecture populaire, tandis que Rasem Badran et d'autres adoptaient une approche historiciste évoquant les grandes réalisations des cultures anciennes, avant la colonisation occidentale. D'autres encore, comme Nira Gandhi en Inde ou Tang Guan Bee à Singapour, ont à leur actif des œuvres intéressantes et éclectiques.

En résumé, on peut dire que depuis les années 50 la production architecturale a connu deux phases. La première introduit le modernisme et le Style International, arrivés en fanfare et restés influents jusque dans les années 80. La seconde comprend des variantes du régionalisme; elle transforme l'architecture populaire et se réfère à l'histoire pour exprimer des identités naissantes. Cette phase prend de l'ampleur au début de la décennie 80, mais elle existait depuis longtemps. Depuis le milieu des années 80, l'architecture asiatique, comme en écho à la profusion offre un large éventail d'expressions dans lesquelles il est difficile de discerner une orientation stylistique.

Le continent asiatique est en plein essor, et ses métropoles brassent des populations de tous les horizons ethniques, sociaux et religieux. En l'an 2000, quinze des vingt villes les plus peuplées de la planète seront en Asie. Les nouvelles technologies, modes d'échange, organisations et les intérêts multinationaux permettent de gérer et de diffuser une expression pluraliste en architecture. Ces aspects multiculturels sont d'ores et déjà du domaine du réel et d'une évidence frappante dans de nombreuses régions d'Asie: le continent est bien placé pour traiter ces nouvelles réalités et pour changer l'ordre du monde au XXIe siècle. Les bouleversements que connaissent les républiques d'Asie centrale, l'émergence des Etats du Sud et de l'Est asiatique en tant qu'acteurs sur la scène internationale et la puissance économique et politique de la Chine sont des faits qui influent sur les événements et les relations des pays de la planète, et par voie de conséquence, sur l'architecture asiatique elle-même.

nalen und asiatischen Identität und mit Problemen der beruflichen Praxis zu befassen. Diese Gruppe bestand aus Fuhimiko Maki und Koichi Nagashima aus Japan, Tao Ho aus Hongkong, William Lim aus Singapur, Sumet Jumsai aus Thailand und Charles Correa aus Indien, die in den achtziger Jahren durchweg Bedeutung erlangt hatten. Diese und andere asiatische Theoretiker, Architekten und Historiker entwickelten ihre Ideen häufig im Rahmen eines Diskurses, der von einflußreichen Kritikern aus dem Westen etabliert wurde.

Während der späten siebziger und achtziger Jahre begannen einige Architekten, den »skin-deep modernism and glib traditionalism« (den oberflächlichen Modernismus und halbherzigen Traditionalismus, um einen Ausdruck von William Curtis zu gebrauchen) neu zu überdenken. Die Versuche, zu einer Synthese zu gelangen, fielen bei den einheimischen und ausländischen Architekten ganz unterschiedlich aus und reflektierten deren persönliche, regionale und internationale Interessen. Sich ausschließlich am Lokalen zu orientieren, war nicht mehr möglich. Zu Anfang der achtziger Jahre versuchten selbst solche Mainstream-Architekten wie Paul Rudolph, Kenzo Tange, I.M. Pei, Foster Associates, um hier nur einige wenige zu nennen, eine Architektur hervorzubringen, die den örtlichen Gegebenheiten, der Zeit, der Kultur und den lokalen Erfordernissen entsprach. Bei ihren früheren Bauten in Asien war dies in der Regel nicht der Fall gewesen.

Einige, wie beispielsweise die Architekten Habib Fida Ali, Won Kim, Tao Ho, blieben der Moderne verhaftet. Andere, wie William Lim, Ken Yeang und Sumet Jumsai, machten sich die Anschauungen der Postmoderne und des Dekonstruktivismus in der Architektur zu eigen. Gleichzeitig arbeiteten Geoffrey Bawa, Laurie Baker und Jimmy Lim weiterhin an der Interpretation des Landestypischen, während Rasem Badran und andere sich bei ihrer Architektur eines historistischen Ansatzes bedienten und sich auf die großartigen Leistungen vergangener Kulturen – vor der Kolonisation durch den Westen – besannen. Wieder andere, so z. B. Nira Gandhi in Indien und Tang Guan Bee in Singapur, haben interessante Bauten geschaffen. Es ist vielleicht nicht ganz fair, die Arbeiten der Architekten

auf diese Weise zu charakterisieren, da sie sich zeitweise auch immer mit anderen Themen befaßt haben, aber es dient hier zur Veranschaulichung der heute in Asien am stärksten vertretenen Tendenzen.

Zusammenfassend läßt sich sagen, daß es seit dem Anfang der fünfziger Jahre zwei Hauptphasen architektonischen Schaffens gegeben hat. In der ersten Phase wurde der Modernismus und der »International Style« eingeführt, der sofort florierte, weiterhin eine starke Rolle spielte und erst in den achtziger Jahren an Bedeutung verlor. In der zweiten Phase wurden, in Abwandlung des einheimischen Baustils, verschiedene Spielarten des Regionalismus integriert, wobei man auf die Geschichte Bezug nahm, um die inzwischen auftretenden Probleme der Identität anzusprechen. Diese Phase setzte sich zu Anfang der achtziger Jahre stärker durch. Fast wie eine Widerspiegelung der Flut von Informationen und Bildern, die inzwischen weltweit übermittelt werden, hat die asiatische Architektur seit Mitte der achtziger Jahre ein breites Spektrum an eklektizistischen Ausdrucksformen hervorgebracht, in denen sich einzelne Stilrichtungen kaum noch ausmachen lassen.

Die Städte Asiens erleben einen bisher nie dagewesenen Größenzuwachs. Bis zum Jahre 2000 werden etwa fünfzehn der zwanzig bevölkerungsreichsten Städte der Welt asiatisch sein, und es werden Menschen verschiedener ethnischer, religiöser und sozialer Herkunft in ihnen leben. Mit Hilfe der neuen Technologien, der Methoden der Übermittlung und der multi-nationalen Organisationen und Konzerne wird die Beherrschung und Verbreitung pluralistischer Ausdrucksformen in der Architektur möglich sein. In vielen Teilen Asiens, das aufgrund seiner Lage prädestiniert ist, sich den neuen Realitäten und der sich verändernden Weltordnung des 21. Jahrhunderts zu stellen, sind diese multi-kulturellen Aspekte schon heute eine Realität und machen sich bereits auf eindrucksvolle Weise bemerkbar. Die tiefgreifenden Veränderungen in den zentralasiatischen Republiken, die Entwicklung der süd- und ostasiatischen Staaten zu Mitspielern im Weltgeschehen sowie die internationale wirtschaftliche und politische Macht Chinas – all das wirkt sich auf die Beziehungen und Ereignisse in der ganzen Welt aus und damit auch auf die asiatische Architektur selbst.

Chee Tong Temple (1987), Singapore,
reinterprets the traditional chinese
roof.

Der Chee Tong Tempel (1987) in Singapur greift das Motiv des traditionellen chinesischen Daches auf.

Le Chee Tong Temple (1987), à Singapour, réinterprète le toit traditionnel
chinois.

Akitekt Tenggara II
Singapore

Started in 1976 by founding principal Tay Kheng Soon, Akitekt Tenggara was initially concerned with low-income public housing. With two semiautonomous offices in Singapore and Kuala Lumpur, it has undertaken commercial, recreational, institutional, and touristic projects. In 1989 Akitekt Tenggara II was formed to take in younger partners, thereby injecting new talent into the firm. Tay believes that good design must make economic sense and that wit can transcend constraints to produce "a surprising result that holds together with integrity". A strong and personable advocate of innovation, Tay remains concerned with regional, climatic, and cultural concerns, and, as a result, his buildings vary from expressions of tradition to high-tech, often producing an elusive ambiguity. His work is often highly intellectual and experimental. He has taught and written about architectural and urban design and continues to be one of the most interesting figures in Asian architecture today.

Ursprünglich war Akitekt Tenggara, 1976 von Tay Kheng Soon gegründet, im sozialen Wohnungsbau tätig. Die beiden halb-autonomen Büros in Singapur und Kuala Lumpur, führten Projekte kommerzieller und institutioneller Art sowie Aufträge in den Bereichen Freizeit und Tourismus aus. 1989 wurde Akitekt Tenggara II gegründet, um auch jüngere Partner mit einzubeziehen, wodurch dem Unternehmen neue Talente zuflossen. Tay ist überzeugt, daß gutes Design ökonomisch Sinn machen muß und daß man durch Einfallsreichtum Zwänge überwinden und so zu »einem überraschenden Ergebnis gelangen kann, das seinen Zusammenhalt in der Einheit findet«. Tay ist ein engagierter Verfechter von Innovationen, berücksichtigt jedoch immer auch die regionalen, klimatischen und kulturellen Bedingungen. Seine Bauten umfassen daher das gesamte Spektrum, von traditionellem Ausdruck bis hin zu High-Tech, wobei häufig eine schwer zu fassende Vieldeutigkeit entsteht. Er lehrte und schrieb über Architektur und Städtebau und ist noch immer einer der interessantesten Vertreter der zeitgenössischen Architektur in Asien.

Créée en 1976 sous la direction de Tay Kheng Soon, l'agence Akitekt Tenggara s'est d'abord consacrée à la construction de logements municipaux bon marché. Puis, avec deux bureaux indépendants à Singapour et à Kuala Lumpur, elle a réalisé des projets commerciaux, institutionnels, touristiques et récréatifs. En 1989, est créée Akitekt Tenggara II qui accueille de jeunes collaborateurs, introduisant par ce moyen de nouveaux talents dans l'entreprise. Tay pense qu'un bon projet est un projet rationnel du point de vue économique, et que l'ingéniosité peut transcender les contraintes pour produire un résultat surprenant de cohérence. Ardent partisan de l'innovation, Tay n'oublie jamais les impératifs régionaux, climatiques et culturels; ses édifices sont donc aussi bien l'expression de la tradition que de la haute technologie, produisant parfois une ambiguïté insaisissable. Son travail est hautement intellectuel et expérimental. Il a enseigné l'architecture, écrit sur l'urbanisme et reste l'une des personnalités les plus intéressantes de l'architecture asiatique contemporaine.

Institute of Technical Education (1993), Bisham, Singapore

This dramatic educational building projects an image of technical progress and responds to the region's tropical climate. Designed as two parallel curved blocks, the 4-storey structure allows for easy transition through its large-span concrete and steel construction. The overhanging roofs offer protection from rain and sun, while the vertical skin is permeable to air. The architectural language is a poetic celebration of technology.

Dieses beeindruckende Ausbildungsgebäude projiziert ein Bild des technischen Fortschritts und korrespondiert mit dem tropischen Klima der Region. Konzipiert als zwei parallele, geschwungene Baukörper, erlaubt der vierstöckige Bau einen leichten Durchgang durch die weit ausladende Beton- und Stahlkonstruktion. Die vorstehenden Dächer bieten Schutz vor Regen und Sonne, die vertikale Außenverkleidung ist dagegen luftdurchlässig. Diese Architektur ist ein Loblied auf die Technologie.

Ce bel établissement d'enseignement projette l'image du progrès technique: deux blocs parallèles incurvés, une construction en acier et béton à grande portée qui facilite la circulation sur les quatre étages de l'ensemble. Tout ici a été pensé en fonction du climat tropical: les toits en surplomb protègent de la pluie et du soleil tandis que le revêtement vertical est perméable à l'air. Le langage architectural est un hymne poétique à la technologie.

View of the internal garden. The 18 metre-wide area separates the two strips of teaching blocks.

Ansicht des Innengartens. Die 18 Meter breite Fläche trennt die beiden Baukörper mit den Unterrichtsgebäuden.

Vue du jardin intérieur. Cet espace de 18 mètres de large sépare deux bâtiments d'enseignement construits en longueur.

General view of the huge vault of the multi-purpose hall at the south end of the complex.

Gesamtansicht des riesigen Gewölbes der Mehrzweckhalle am südlichen Ende des Komplexes.

Vue d'ensemble de la haute voûte du hall multifonctions dans la partie sud du complexe.

An open, canopied auditorium just inside the entrance acts as a central meeting point. The glass lift tower connects the galleries and other spaces on either side.

Ein offenes, mit einem Baldachin überdachtes Auditorium direkt im Eingangsbereich dient als zentraler Treffpunkt. Der gläserne Aufzugsturm schafft eine Verbindung zwischen den Galerien und den übrigen Räumen auf beiden Seiten.

Le hall d'entrée, ouvert et recouvert d'une voûte protectrice, sert de point de rencontre. La tour d'ascenseur en verre relie de part et d'autre les galeries et d'autres espaces.

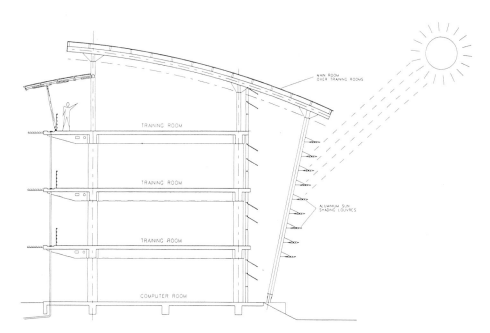

Schematic section through the shading devices.

Schematischer Schnitt, der das System der Sonnenschutzvorrichtungen darstellt.

Coupe transversale montrant le système de brise-soleil.

Site plan showing the ground floor layout.

Lageplan mit dem Grundriß des Erdgeschosses.

Plan du rez-de-chaussée.

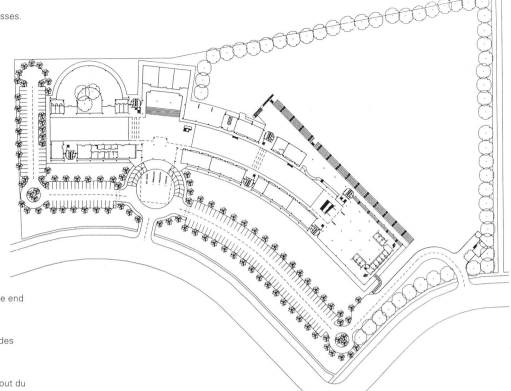

The entrance to the multi-purpose hall at the end
of the complex.

Der Eingang zur Mehrzweckhalle am Ende des
Komplexes.

Entrée menant au hall polyvalent situé au bout du
complexe.

Atelier 6
Indonesia

The firm Atelier 6 (or Enam), a loose association of six partners, is one of the most successful practises in Indonesia. The partner-directors, each of whose approach to design varies considerably, control their own projects and share backup services, staff, and office space. The directors are often involved in other cultural, academic, or business activities as well. Adhi Moersid, one of the directors, has been concerned with interpreting traditional architecture "to reconstruct a series of components with symbolic content". This can be seen in many of his works, although his urban high-rise commercial buildings are often in the International Style usually demanded by his corporate clients. In his institutional buildings, in which the expression of modernity is a primary concern, he introduces local elements to produce hybrid buildings that reflect the country's general preoccupation with retaining tradition in a contemporary and rapidly modernizing society. His works continue to be diverse and eclectic in their expression while referring to Javanese forms and symbols.

Atelier 6 (oder Enam) ist ein loser Zusammenschluß von sechs Partnern und gehört zu den erfolgreichsten Architekturbüros in Indonesien. Die Partner sind häufig auch an anderen kulturellen, universitären oder geschäftlichen Aktivitäten beteiligt. Adhi Moersid, einer der Partner, beschäftigt sich mit der Interpretation traditioneller Bauwerke, »um einige Elemente von symbolischer Bedeutung neu zu gestalten«. Dies wird an vielen seiner Arbeiten sichtbar, wenngleich seine städtischen, kommerziellen Hochhausbauten oft im »International Style« gebaut sind, wie von den Auftraggebern gewünscht. Bei seinen öffentlichen Gebäuden, bei denen es in erster Linie um den Ausdruck von Modernität geht, läßt er auch lokale Elemente mit einfließen, so daß in seiner Architektur eine Mischung entsteht, in der sich das allgemeine Interesse des Landes widerspiegelt, in einer sich rasch modernisierenden Gesellschaft an der Tradition dennoch festzuhalten. Seine Bauten bleiben in ihrem Ausdruck vielfältig und eklektizistisch, greifen dabei aber auf javanische Formen und Symbole zurück.

L'Atelier 6 (ou Enam), association libre de six architectes, est l'un des cabinets les plus prospères d'Indonésie. Chaque associé conserve son approche personnelle de l'architecture, contrôle ses propres projets et partage les services auxiliaires, le personnel et les bureaux de l'agence. Les associés ont souvent des activités dans le domaine de la culture ou de l'enseignement, ou même dans les affaires. Adhi Moersid, l'un de ces architectes, se consacre à l'interprétation de l'architecture traditionnelle «pour reconstruire une série de composantes à contenu symbolique». Cette approche est perceptible dans son travail bien que ses hautes constructions à usage commercial empruntent au Style international, une exigence de ses clients. Dans ses édifices institutionnels, où l'expression de la modernité est la préoccupation essentielle, il introduit des éléments locaux pour créer des structures hybrides, reflets du désir de conserver la tradition dans une société contemporaine en pleine modernisation. Ses réalisations sont d'une expression variée et éclectique tout en faisant référence aux formes et aux symboles javanais.

A modern office building (1991) in Jakarta differs from the firm's work with traditional models.

Ein modernes Bürogebäude in Jakarta (1991). Es unterscheidet sich von den anderen Bauten dieses Architektenteams, die auf traditionelle Vorbilder zurückgreifen.

Immeuble de bureaux moderne (1991) à Djakarta. Il diffère des autres réalisations de ce cabinet d'architectes, qui reprennent des formes traditionnelles.

Entrance view of the renovated house.

Vorderansicht des renovierten Hauses.

Vue de l'entrée de la maison rénovée.

Sardono House
(1992), Jakarta

Sardono Kusomo, a prominent dancer and choreographer, asked Moersid to renovate an existing house in Kemang, South Jakarta. Working in close collaboration with the owner, the architect re-arranged the rooms around a small rear courtyard and added an upper floor studio. The house has an airy, open feel with rooms around a garden court.

Sardono Kusomo, ein prominenter Tänzer und Choreograph bat Moersid, ein schon bestehendes Haus in Kemang, im Süden Jakartas, zu renovieren. In enger Zusammenarbeit mit dem Eigentümer, legte der Architekt die Räume rund um einen kleinen, nach hinten gelegenen Innenhof neu an und baute oben noch zusätzlich ein Atelier ein. Das Haus, dessen Zimmer um einen Innenhof mit Garten liegen, strahlt eine luftige, offene Atmosphäre aus.

Sardono Kusomo, danseur, chorégraphe très en vue, a chargé Moersid de rénover sa maison de Kemang dans le Sud de Djakarta. La rénovation fut le fruit d'une collaboration étroite entre le propriétaire et l'architecte. Moersid réaménagea les pièces autour de la petite cour arrière et souleva la maison d'un étage pour y installer un studio. Les pièces disposées autour du jardin intérieur donnent une impression de fluidité et d'espace.

The *pendopo*, or pavilion, off the small rear garden courtyard, is used as a traditional space for greeting guests. It is also used as a music room.

Der *pendopo*, oder Pavillon, der sich auf den kleinen hinteren Gartenhof öffnet, ist der traditionelle Raum zur Begrüßung der Gäste und wird auch als Musikzimmer genutzt.

Le pavillon – le *pendopo* – donnant sur le petit jardin arrière sert de lieu d'accueil traditionnel des hôtes. Il sert aussi de salle de musique.

The living room forms a wing surrounded on three sides by a garden.

Das Wohnzimmer bildet einen Flügel, der an drei Seiten von einem Garten umgeben ist.

Le salon forme une aile entourée sur trois côtés par le jardin.

Carita Beach Resort (1993), Banten, West Java

Built as a large seaside holiday village, the resort has much in common with other such developments in Southeast Asia. It consists of a central building with public areas and guest rooms, a series of individual cottages, sports and recreational facilities, and interlinked swimming pools set adjacent to the beach. The complex uses the local Javanese vernacular with its tiled roofs, low buildings and pavilions set within lush landscaped gardens.

Erbaut im Stile eines großen Feriendorfes am Meer, hat dieser Erholungsort viel mit vergleichbaren anderen Entwicklungen in Südostasien gemeinsam. Er besteht aus einem zentralen Bau mit öffentlich zugänglichen Bereichen, Gästezimmern, einer Reihe von individuellen, kleinen Ferienhäusern, Sportplätzen und Freizeiteinrichtungen sowie angeschlossenen Swimmingpools, die in der Nähe des Strandes liegen. Der Baukomplex bedient sich des lokalen javanischen Baustils mit seinen Ziegeldächern, Flachbauten und Pavillons, die in eine üppige Gartenlandschaft hineingebaut sind.

Construite comme un grand village de vacances au bord de la mer, cette station balnéaire a beaucoup de points communs avec les autres installations touristiques d'Asie du Sud-Est. Elle se compose d'un bâtiment central abritant les espaces publics et les chambres, d'une série de petites maisons individuelles, d'installations sportives et récréatives, et enfin de plusieurs piscines reliées entre elles et jouxtant la plage. L'architecture s'inspire du style javanais local avec ses toits en tuiles, ses constructions basses et ses pavillons nichés dans des jardins à la végétation luxuriante.

Right: The hotel seen from the swimming pool area.
Bottom: Rooms, each with its own balcony, overlook the richly landscaped gardens.
Page 67 bottom: The large pool area around the hotel.

Rechts: Blick von der Swimmingpool-Anlage auf das Hotel.
Unten: Die Räume, die jeweils einen eigenen Balkon haben, geben den Blick frei auf die üppigen Gärten.
Seite 67 unten: Die große, um das Hotel herum gebaute Swimmingpool-Anlage.

A droite: L'hôtel vu depuis la piscine.
Ci-dessous: Les chambres, toutes dotées de balcon, donnent sur les jardins magnifiquement aménagés.
Page 67 en bas: Le vaste espace de la piscine autour de l'hôtel.

Geoffrey Bawa
Sri Lanka

Three Buddhist temple pavilions (1977) are built on a small island in the Beira Lake, Colombo. Seen here is the central pavilion where priests are ordained. The timber structure and overhanging tiled roof are characteristic of Bawa's work.

Drei buddhistische Tempel-Pavillons (1977) auf einer kleinen Insel im Beira Lake, Colombo. Hier der zentrale Pavillon, in dem die Priester ordiniert werden. Die Holzkonstruktion und das überhängende Ziegeldach sind typisch für Bawas Werk.

Trois temple-pavillons bouddhistes (1977) construits sur un îlot de Beira Lake, Colombo. On peut apercevoir ici le pavillon central où les prêtres sont ordonnés. La construction en bois et le toit de tuile en saillie sont caractéristiques de l'œuvre de Bawa.

Geoffrey Bawa is one of the finest architects in the world today. Highly personal in his approach, evoking the pleasures of the senses that go hand in hand with the climate, landscape, and culture of ancient Ceylon, Bawa brings together an appreciation of the Western humanist tradition in architecture with needs and lifestyles of his own country. Although Bawa came to practise his profession only at the age of 38 (he was a lawyer first), his buildings over the last 25 or more years are widely acclaimed in Sri Lanka, from his more recent parliament buildings and a university to private houses, hotels, and schools. The intense devotion he brings to composing his architecture in an intimate relationship with nature is witnessed by his attention to landscape and vegetation, the crucial setting for his architecture. His sensitivity to environment is reflected in his careful attention to the sequencing of space, the creation of vistas, courtyards, and walkways, the use of materials and treatment of details.

Geoffrey Bawa ist heute einer der bedeutendsten Architekten der Welt. Mit seinem sehr persönlichen Stil, der die Sinnesfreuden, die mit dem Klima, der Landschaft und der Kultur des altehrwürdigen Ceylon einhergehen, wachruft, gelingt Bawa eine Synthese aus der Wertschätzung der westlichen, humanistischen Architekturtradition und den Bedürfnissen und Lebensformen seines eigenen Landes. Obwohl Bawa zur Ausübung seines Berufes erst im Alter von 38 kam (er war zuvor Rechtsanwalt), finden seine Bauten der letzten 25 oder mehr Jahre großen Beifall in Sri Lanka, angefangen bei seinen, erst vor kurzem gebauten Parlamentsgebäuden über eine Universität bis hin zu den Privathäusern, Hotels und Schulen. Mit welcher Hingabe er seine Bauten in eine enge Beziehung zur Natur setzt, zeigt sich an der sorgsamen Beachtung der Landschaft und Vegetation, die seiner Architektur den entscheidenden Rahmen geben. Sein hochentwickelter Sinn für Umgebung spiegelt sich in der sorgfältig geplanten Anordnung der Räume, der Konzipierung von Aussichten, Innenhöfen und Gehwegen, dem Einsatz von Materialien und der Behandlung von Details.

Geoffrey Bawa est l'un des meilleurs architectes de notre époque. Très personnel dans son approche évocatrice des plaisirs des sens allant de pair avec le climat, le paysage et la culture de l'ancienne Ceylan, Bawa réussit à marier avec bonheur la tradition humaniste occidentale et les besoins et le style de vie de son pays. Cet ancien avocat devenu architecte à l'âge de 38 ans réalise depuis un quart de siècle des projets qui sont salués unanimement au Sri Lanka, que ce soit le Parlement, l'université, des maisons, des hôtels ou des écoles. La ferveur qu'il met à composer son architecture en relation intime avec la nature révèle son attention pour le paysage et la végétation, cadre dominant de son architecture. Sa sensibilité à l'environnement se reflète dans le soin attentif qu'il accorde aux séquences spatiales, à la création de perspectives, de cours et de passages, à l'usage des matériaux et au traitement des détails.

Top: The physics building and lecture hall situated
on different levels.

Oben: Das Physik-Gebäude und der Hörsaal, die auf
verschiedenen Ebenen liegen.

Ci-dessus: Le bâtiment de physique et
l'amphithéâtre s'étagent sur des niveaux différents.

Bottom: Elevation of the university viewed from the
sea and approach road.

Unten: Ansicht der Universität, vom Meer und der
Zufahrtsstraße aus gesehen.

Ci-dessous: Elévation des bâtiments de l'université
depuis la mer et la route d'accès.

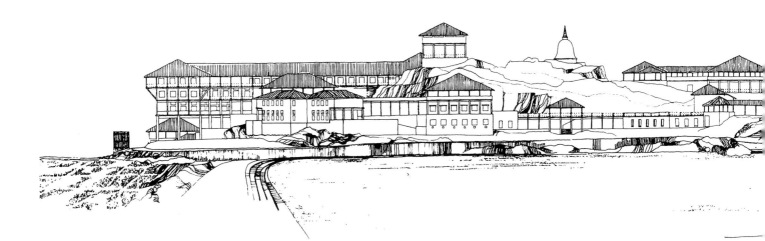

University of Ruhunu (1980–86), Matara

A spectacular hilly site on the southern coast overlooking the sea was chosen for the arts & sciences faculties of a new university for 5 000 students. The complex consists of a series of buildings linked by terraces, gardens, and covered walkways that give space for pause, contemplation, and meetings. The modestly elegant buildings of different heights are carefully placed in the landscape to create a pleasing academic atmosphere.

Für die Geistes- und Naturwissenschaftlichen Fakultäten einer neuen Universität für 5 000 Studenten wurde eine beeindruckende Hügellage mit Blick auf das Meer gewählt. Der Komplex besteht aus einer Reihe von Gebäuden, die durch Terrassen, Gärten und überdachte Gehwege verbunden sind, die genügend Raum zum Innehalten, Nachdenken und für Begegnungen bieten. Die eleganten Gebäude unterschiedlicher Höhe sind mit Sorgfalt in die Landschaft gestellt, so daß eine angenehme Studienatmosphäre entsteht.

Pour construire les facultés des lettres et des sciences d'une nouvelle université accueillant 5 000 étudiants, les autorités choisirent sur la côte méridionale un très beau site vallonné dominant la mer. Ce complexe universitaire se compose d'une série de bâtiments reliés par des terrasses, des jardins et des passages couverts, offrant ainsi des espaces pour les pauses, les rencontres et la contemplation. Les bâtiments, sobrement élégants créent une atmosphère studieuse.

A classroom block overlooking a courtyard and connected to other buildings by a walkway.

Ein Komplex mit Unterrichtsräumen, der den Blick auf einen Innenhof freigibt und mit den übrigen Gebäuden durch einen Gehweg verbunden ist.

Ensemble de salles de cours surplombant une cour et reliées à d'autres bâtiments par passage couvert.

View from the lobby to the pool and the sea, just after a thunderstorm.

Blick aus der Hotelhalle auf den Pool und das Meer, unmittelbar nach einem Gewitter.

Vue de la piscine et de la mer depuis le hall, juste après un orage.

Page 73: View of the entrance façade with its coconut tree pool.

Seite 73: Ansicht der Eingangsfassade mit dem Teich und seinen Kokospalmen.

Page 73: Vue de la façade de l'entrée avec son plan d'eau aux cocotiers.

Triton Hotel (1982), Ahungalla

Located on the southwestern coast of Sri Lanka, the hotel's 130 guest rooms are strung along the beach. Bawa introduced playful elements into the design, such as the large ornamental pool at the entry driveway, the U-shaped courtyards, and the lobby, which opens onto the swimming pool beside the sea; all create a landscape within a landscape. This is one of his most easily decipherable and visually stimulating works.

An der Südwestküste von Sri Lanka gelegen, sind die 130 Gästezimmer des Hotels entlang dem Strand gebaut. Bawa hat auch spielerische Elemente in seinen Entwurf integriert, so z.B. den großen, dekorativen Teich nahe der Auffahrt, die U-förmigen Innenhöfe und die Vorhalle, die sich zum Swimmingpool am Meer hin öffnet, wodurch nochmals eine Landschaft innerhalb der Landschaft geschaffen wird. Dies ist eines der am leichtesten zu entziffernden und visuell anregendsten Werke.

Situé sur la côte du sud-ouest du Sri Lanka, cet hôtel de 130 chambres a été construit le long de la plage. Bawa a intégré dans le plan des éléments ludiques tels que la grande pièce d'eau ornementale, point d'aboutissement de l'allée de l'entrée, les cours en forme de U et le hall donnant sur la piscine côté mer; tous ces éléments créent un paysage dans le paysage. Cet hôtel est l'une de ses réalisations les plus faciles à déchiffrer et les plus stimulantes sur le plan visuel.

Stairs to the upper level with a mural by Laki Senayake.

Treppenaufgang zum Obergeschoß, mit einem Wandbild von Laki Senayake.

Escalier menant à l'étage supérieur et peinture murale de Laki Senayake.

Right: The pool and sea seen from one of the guest bedrooms.

Rechts: Blick von einem der Gästeschlafzimmer auf den Pool und das Meer.

A droite: La piscine et la mer vues d'une chambre de l'hôtel.

Page 74: View from the rooms with a seaview.

Seite 74: Blick aus einem der Zimmer mit Aussicht auf das Meer.

Page 74: Vue de la mer depuis les chambres.

BEEAH: Hussaini-Shuaibi
Saudi Arabia

Abdul Rahman Hussaini

Ali Shuaibi

The Sapico office building (1990) in Islamabad is jointly designed by BEEAH and Nayyar Ali Dada. It recalls Mughal architecture in its massing and its blue tilework.

Das Sapico-Bürogebäude (1990) in Islamabad von BEEAH und Nayyar Ali Dada erinnert durch seine Form und die tiefblauen Kacheln an den Mughal-Baustil.

L'immeuble Sapico (1990) d'Islamabad de BEEAH et de Nayyar Ali Dada. La masse et les faïences décoratives bleu outremer évoquent irrésistiblement l'architecture moghole.

One of the best-known firms in Saudi Arabia, BEEAH (meaning "total environment" in Arabic) was founded in 1975 and has endured to produce a wide range of essentially modernist buildings. The architectural partnership has achieved prominence for its institutional and governmental projects and for its attention to landscaping in a country that has very little of this tradition. The partners, Abdul Rahman Hussaini and Ali Shuaibi, are jointly responsible for the design of all projects. Their knowledge of their own culture and country has led them to modify their approach to take into account local conditions, which they have done successfully even in their earlier projects. In their later works the layout and detailing of the buildings increase in sophistication. BEEAH has won numerous international and local competitions and awards. The partnership is becoming an important voice for Arab and Asian architecture.

Eines der bekanntesten Unternehmen in Saudi-Arabien, BEEAH (was in arabischer Sprache so viel bedeutet wie »vollständige Umwelt«) wurde 1975 gegründet und hat seither ein breites Spektrum überwiegend modernistischer Bauwerke geschaffen. Das Architekturbüro ist bekannt für seine Behörden- und Regierungsprojekte und für seine besonderen Bemühungen um die Landschaftsgestaltung in einem Land, das auf diesem Sektor kaum eine Tradition hat. Die Partner, Abdul Rahman Hussaini und Ali Shuaibi, tragen die gemeinsame Verantwortung für sämtliche Projekt-Entwürfe. Ihre Kenntnis der eigenen Kultur und des Landes hat sie dazu veranlaßt, ihren theoretischen Ansatz zu modifizieren und auch lokale Gegebenheiten mit zu berücksichtigen, etwas, das sie auch in ihren früheren Projekten bereits mit Erfolg praktiziert haben. In ihren späteren Werken gewinnen Anlage und Detailausgestaltung noch an technischer Perfektion. BEEAH hat zahlreiche internationale und lokale Wettbewerbe sowie Preise gewonnen. Diese Gruppe ist dabei, zu einem wichtigen Sprachrohr für die arabische und asiatische Architektur zu werden.

BEEAH («environnement total» en arabe), l'une des agences les plus connues d'Arabie Saoudite, a été fondée en 1975 et compte à son actif un grand éventail d'édifices en majeure partie modernistes. Cette association d'architectes occupe une place importante grâce à ses projets institutionnels et gouvernementaux ainsi qu'à l'attention qu'elle accorde à l'aménagement paysager dans un pays où la tradition fait défaut en la matière. Les associés, Abdul Rahman Hussaini (formé à Riyad) et Ali Shuaibi (formé à Riyad et aux Etats-Unis), conçoivent ensemble leurs projets. Leur connaissance du pays et de sa culture les a conduits à modifier leur approche et à tenir compte des conditions locales. Ils l'ont fait avec succès même dans leurs premiers projets. Dans les réalisations suivantes, le dessin et les détails gagnèrent en sophistication. BEEAH a remporté de nombreux prix et concours, régionaux ou internationaux. Cette association apparaît de plus en plus comme un des porteparole de l'architecture arabe et asiatique.

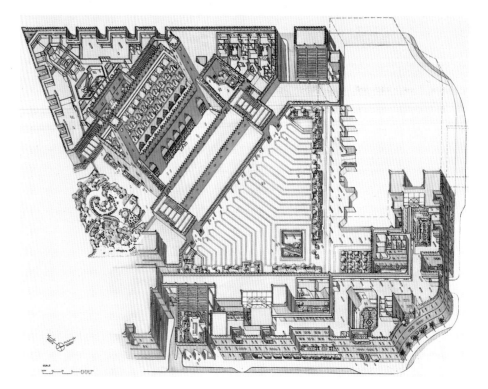

Cutaway axonometric view of the Al-Kindi area showing the mosque to the west of the central plaza, and the government offices to the northeast.

Axonometrischer Ausschnitt des Al-Kindi-Viertels, mit der Moschee im Westen des zentralen Marktplatzes und den Regierungsgebäuden im Nordosten.

Vue axonométrique du secteur d'Al-Kindi montrant la mosquée à l'ouest de la place centrale et les bureaux administratifs au nord-est.

Page 79: Seen from the plaza, the sand-coloured walls of the entrance to the mosque use the angular vocabulary of Najd buildings.

Seite 79: Blick vom Marktplatz aus; für die sandfarbenen Mauern des Eingangs zur Moschee ist das winklige Vokabular der Najd-Bauten verwendet worden.

Page 79: Vue de la mosquée depuis la place: les murs de l'entrée reprennent le vocabulaire angulaire des constructions Najd.

Al-Kindi Area
(1981–86), Diplomatic Quarter, Riyadh

The Diplomatic Quarter is a major urban development scheme that has been partially completed. The core of the area, Al-Kindi, comprises the *jami*, or Friday Mosque, and government office complexes, in addition to commercial, recreational, and parking facilities over 26,000 square meters of land with twice as much built-up area. The buildings form a contiguous mass around the Al-Kindi plaza and are suitably designed for the hot, dry climate, following the Najd architectural style and using modern construction technology. The work, which won an Aga Khan Award for Architecture in 1989, makes an important contribution to the region's architecture.

Das Diplomatenviertel ist ein großes städtebauliches Projekt, das bereits teilweise abgeschlossen ist. Sein Kernstück, Al-Kindi, umfaßt den *jami*, oder die Friday Mosque (Freitags-Moschee), die Regierungsgebäude sowie Geschäfte, Freizeiteinrichtungen und Parkplätze auf 26 000 Quadratmetern und einer bebauten Fläche doppelten Umfangs. Die Bauten bilden eine den Al-Kindi-Platz umgrenzende Einheit und sind, dem heißen und trockenen Klima entsprechend, im Najd-Baustil und unter Verwendung moderner Bautechniken errichtet worden. Dieses Projekt, das 1989 mit dem Aga Khan Award for Architecture ausgezeichnet wurde, stellt für die Architektur dieser Region einen wichtigen Beitrag dar.

L'enceinte diplomatique est un grand programme de développement urbain en partie achevé. Au cœur de ce quartier appelé Al-Kindi se trouvent la *jami* (mosquée du vendredi) et les bâtiments administratifs, les commerces, les installations récréatives et les parkings, couvrant 26 000 m² de terrain avec le double de domaine bâti. Les édifices, qui forment une masse continue autour de la place Al-Kindi, sont conçus pour un climat chaud et sec. Ils sont dans le style Najd et ont été construits avec des moyens technologiques modernes. Cette réalisation, qui a reçu le Prix Aga Khan en 1989, a beaucoup apporté à l'architecture de la région.

The government services building seen from the main boulevard.

Der Komplex der Regierungsbehörden, von der Hauptstraße aus gesehen.

Les bureaux administratifs vus depuis le grand boulevard.

Atrium of the government services building.

Atrium des Regierungsgebäudes.

Atrium du bâtiment administratif.

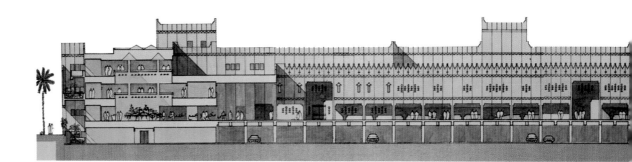

Section through the *jami* (Friday Mosque) and the
government services office; elevation of the shops
adjacent to the plaza.

Schnitt der *jami* (Freitags-Moschee) und der
Regierungsbehörden; Aufriß der an den Marktplatz
angrenzenden Läden.

Coupe de la *jami* (mosquée du vendredi) et des
bureaux administratifs; élévation des boutiques
adjacentes à la place.

Turgut Cansever
Turkey

Turgut Cansever is Turkey's most important living architect. His work over the years reveals a consistent concern with building traditions and vocabulary related to context. He is the only architect to have won the prestigious Aga Khan Award for Architecture on three occasions (for the buildings illustrated here). His architecture usually echoes its surroundings in its massing, use of materials, and details: however, he does not copy the past but produces a new architecture around a basic archetypal syntax. In this way, the buildings themselves present a discourse. In addition to his design sensibility and care, his use of materials and the articulation of his work manifest a craftsman-like precision. Not only a practitioner, he has thought and written about architecture with special emphasis on the religion and culture of Islam. While his production is not so prolific and he is not yet widely known, he makes an important contribution toward a synthesis of the historical, the vernacular, and the modernist.

Turgut Cansever ist der bedeutendste Architekt der Türkei. In seinen Arbeiten zeigt sich ein beständiges Interesse an Bautraditionen und einem kontextbezogenen Vokabular. Er ist der einzige Architekt, dem bei drei verschiedenen Anlässen (für die hier abgebildeten Bauten) der prestigeträchtige Aga Khan Award for Architecture verliehen wurde. Seine Bauten reflektieren ihre Umgebung meist durch die Art ihrer Zusammenstellung und die Verwendung von Materialien und Details. Dabei kopiert er jedoch die Vergangenheit nicht, sondern bringt einen neuen Baustil hervor. Neben seinem Sinn für Formen und seiner Sorgfalt manifestiert sich in der Verwendung von Materialien und der Gliederung seiner Bauten eine fast handwerkliche Präzision. Er ist aber nicht nur Praktiker, sondern hat sich auch theoretisch mit der Architektur, insbesondere mit der Religion und Kultur des Islam, befaßt und darüber publiziert. Obwohl sein Werk noch nicht so umfangreich und er noch nicht so bekannt ist, leistet er bereits einen wichtigen Beitrag zur Entwicklung einer Synthese aus Historischem, Ortstypischem und Modernem.

Turgut Cansever est le plus grand architecte actuel de Turquie. Son œuvre révèle un intérêt constant pour les traditions du bâtiment et un vocabulaire lié au contexte. Il est le seul architecte à avoir reçu trois fois le Prix Aga Khan (pour les édifices ici représentés). L'architecture qu'il crée se fait l'écho de son cadre par ses masses et son usage des matériaux et des détails; sans jamais copier le passé, Cansever produit une nouvelle architecture avec une syntaxe de base archétype, et en ce sens, on peut dire que les constructions sont elles-mêmes un discours. L'attention au détail, l'utilisation des matériaux et l'articulation des espaces révèlent la précision de l'artisan. Cansever n'est pas seulement un praticien: c'est aussi un théoricien qui a réfléchi et écrit sur l'architecture, avec un intérêt particulier pour l'Islam en tant que religion et que culture. Quoique encore peu nombreuses et mal connues, ses réalisations ont beaucoup contribué à la synthèse du modernisme et de l'architecture vernaculaire et historique.

The Ertegun House (1973) in Bodrum on the Turkish coast was remodeled and extended by Cansever.

Das Ertegun Haus (1973) in Bodrum an der türkischen Küste wurde von Cansever um- und ausgebaut.

La Ertegun House (1973) à Bodrum sur la côte turque. Elle a été remodelée et agrandie par Cansever.

Demir Holiday Village
(1987 and ongoing), near Bodrum

The village consists of 35 villas on a 50-hectare site located nine kilometres from Bodrum. The architect (who was also one of the developers) custom-designed each house with a paramount concern for protecting the environment and the beautiful site. The architecture is harmonious with the natural surroundings and uses a common language and construction of stone, wood, and exposed concrete. The wonder of these villas is the architect's skill in layout and the achievement of great variety within the intentionally limited palette of style and materials.

Das Dorf besteht aus 35 Landhäusern auf einem 50 Hektar großen Gelände, neun Kilometer von Bodrum entfernt. Der Architekt (der auch zu den Stadtplanern gehörte), hat die einzelnen Häuser nach den Angaben der Kunden entworfen, wobei er starken Wert auf die Schonung der Umwelt gelegt hat. Seine Architektur fügt sich harmonisch in die natürliche Umgebung ein und basiert auf einer einheitlichen Sprache und Bauweise, die mit Stein, Holz und unverkleidetem Beton arbeitet. Hier zeigt sich der Sinn des Architekten für das Arrangement und die Erzielung einer großen Variationsbreite innerhalb einer bewußt gewählten Beschränkung auf eine bestimmte Anzahl von Stilen und Materialien.

Le village comprend 35 villas sur un terrain de 50 hectares situé à neuf kilomètres de Bodrum. L'architecte (qui était également l'un des promoteurs) dessina chaque maison sur commande avec une préoccupation constante: protéger l'environnement et le site magnifique. L'architecture s'harmonise bien avec le cadre naturel et utilise un langage commun et des matériaux bruts comme la pierre, le bois et le béton apparent. Le plus étonnant dans ces villas, c'est d'abord le dessin qui témoigne de l'habileté de l'architecte, ensuite, la réalisation d'une grande diversité dans une palette de matériaux et de styles volontairement économe.

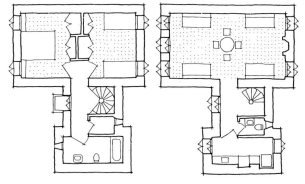

Ground and first floor plans of one of the nine villa types. This two-bedroom unit has a floor area of about 100 square meters.

Grundrisse des Erd- und Obergeschosses eines der neun Ferienhausmodelle. Diese aus zwei Schlafzimmern bestehende Baueinheit hat eine Geschoßfläche von ca. 100 Quadratmetern.

Plans du premier et du second niveaux de l'un des neuf types de maisons. La surface de cette villa de trois pièces est de 100 m² environ.

The landscaping and detailing of each villa is handled with customary care.

Die Landschaftsgestaltung und die Details der Villen wurden mit Sorgfalt ausgeführt.

Chaque détail de l'aménagement paysager et des maisons révèle un souci d'élégance et de qualité.

Right: General view of the clustered stone-clad units in the wooded site.

Rechts: Gesamtansicht der zwanglos angeordneten und mit Stein verkleideten Häuser auf dem bewaldeten Gelände.

A droite: Vue d'ensemble des maisons en pierre dans leur site boisé.

A villa overlooking the sea. The masonry construction techniques were developed to shorten construction time and reduce costs.

Eines der Häuser mit Blick auf das Meer. Die spezifischen Mauertechniken wurden zur Verkürzung der Bauarbeiten und Senkung der Baukosten entwickelt.

Une villa surplombant la mer. On développa exprès les techniques de maçonnerie afin de raccourcir la durée de la construction et d'en réduire les coûts.

The low-income housing scheme in
Belapur (1986), New Bombay. It combines the principles: inclusion of
expansion areas; access to public
facilities; participation in forming
one's own environment; the capacity
to conduct income-producing-
activities and spaces open to the sky.

Soziales Wohnungsbauprojekt in
Belapur (1986), New Bombay. Mögli-
che Erweiterungszonen, Zugang zu
öffentlichen Einrichtungen, eine
Beteiligung der Bewohner an der
Gestaltung ihrer Umwelt und die
Möglichkeit zu gewerblichen Aktivitäten sowie freier Raum werden hier
als Correas Prinzipien vereint.

Le projet d'habitations à loyer modéré
de Belapur (1986), à New Bombay. On
y retrouve tous les thèmes chers à
Correa: inclusion de zones d'expansion, égalité d'accès aux infrastructu-
res collectives, participation de la
population à la création de son environnement, implantation locale
d'activités génératrices de revenus,
espaces à ciel ouvert.

Charles **Correa**
India

Charles Correa is a major international figure in architecture and planning, as both as a practitioner and theoretician. His intelligent design response to climate and location is evident in his work, as is his attention to movement through space and changes of light. His concern for the living conditions of India's poor led him to regard people and space as resources, and he has devised many schemes for low-rise, high-density housing intended to provide equity in the built environment. He has written eloquently about housing and town planning and has sought to demonstrate his ideas in developing New Bombay. Correa moves easily from housing for the underprivileged to hotels, public office and cultural centres. His creative use of imagery to project a central idea has marked much of his recent work. His flair for the dramatic is matched by his interest in universal models as represented by *mandalas* (Hindu or Buddhist cosmic diagrams), literally interpreted in his buildings to express the "deep structures of our cultures".

Charles Correa ist einer der führenden Vertreter in der Architektur und Stadtplanung, als Praktiker ebenso wie als Theoretiker. Seine Bauten zeigen, wie geschickt seine Entwürfe auf das Klima und die jeweilige Lage zugeschnitten sind, und verraten einen Sinn für Dynamik, die er durch räumliche Anordnung und wechselnde Lichtverhältnisse erzielt. Er hat zahlreiche Projektentwürfe für Flachbauten in dicht besiedelten Wohngebieten erstellt, die für gerechtere Wohnverhältnisse sorgen sollen. Er hat eloquent über Wohnungsbau und Stadtplanung geschrieben und war bemüht, seine Vorstellungen im Rahmen der Stadtentwicklung New Bombays umzusetzen. Correa wechselt mühelos zwischen dem Bau von Wohnhäusern für die Unterpriviligierten und dem von Hotels, öffentlichen Gebäuden und Kulturzentren. Seine schöpferische Verwendung von Bildhaftem, um eine Idee zu evozieren, ist ein Kennzeichen vieler seiner neu entstandenen Bauten. Er interessiert sich für universelle Konzepte, wie sie in den *mandalas* (hinduistischen oder buddhistischen Diagrammen) dargestellt werden und die in seinen Bauten buchstäblich interpretiert werden.

Charles Correa est un grand théoricien et praticien de l'architecture et de l'urbanisme. Ses réalisations, parfaitement adaptées au climat et au site, revèlent une passion pour le mouvement et les jeux de lumière. Ses préoccupations sociales l'ont amené à créer des ensembles aérés de petits immeubles destinés aux populations défavorisées. Il a écrit avec éloquence sur les questions du logement et de l'urbanisme et cherche à concrétiser ses idées dans le développement du Nouveau Bombay. Mais Charles Correa dessine avec un égal bonheur des hôtels, des bâtiments administratifs et des centres culturels. Sa manière inventive d'exprimer une idée centrale à partir d'images est l'un des traits marquants de ses dernières réalisations. Notons également la présence dans l'œuvre de Correa des *mandalas* bouddhiques qui, dit l'architecte, expriment les «structures profondes de nos cultures».

The amphitheatre has its own entrance at the top of the step-seats, an open roof overlooks the museum courts.

Das Amphitheater hat einen eigenen Eingang; oberhalb der Stufen-Sitze befindet sich ein offenes Dach, von dem man in die einzelnen Höfe des Museums herunter blickt.

L'amphithéâtre a sa propre entrée; en haut des gradins, un toit ouvert donne sur les cours du musée.

Bottom: Ground floor plan.

Unten: Grundriß des Erdgeschosses.

Ci-dessous: Plan du rez-de-chaussée.

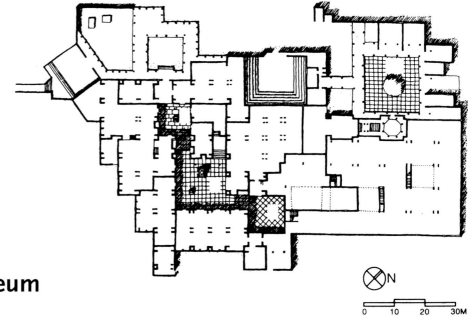

N

| 0 | 10 | 20 | 30M |

National Crafts Museum (1975–91), Delhi

The museum is arranged as a sequence of spaces and courtyards linked together by internal streets. The large permanent collection of folk and tribal arts, crafts, and textiles is housed in low concrete structures modeled on village-scale units. The building resists the notion of a museum by presenting an almost 'everyday experience' that is socially and artistically gratifying. The complex also contains a handicrafts village where works are produced for sale; the whole represents living Indian traditions.

Das Museum ist als eine Folge von Räumen und Innenhöfen angelegt, die durch intern verlaufende Straßen miteinander verbunden sind. Die umfangreiche Dauerkollektion von Objekten der Volks- und Stammeskunst, von kunstgewerblichen Gegenständen und Textilien, ist in flachen Betonbauten untergebracht, die in Stil und Größe denen eines Dorfes entsprechen. Man mag das Gebäude nicht recht als Museum bezeichnen, da hier eine fast »alltägliche Erfahrung« präsentiert wird. Der Komplex umfaßt auch ein Dorf mit handwerklicher Kunst, in dem Arbeiten für den Verkauf hergestellt werden.

Le musée s'articule en une séquence d'espaces et de cours reliés par un système de rues intérieures. La collection permanente d'art, d'artisanat et de textiles populaires et tribaux est présentée dans des bâtiments en béton qui reprennent l'échelle des unités villageoises. La construction ne correspond pas exactement à l'idée de musée car c'est une «expérience de tous les jours» ou presque, très agréable sur le plan social et artistique, qui y est proposée. Le centre comprend aussi un village d'artisans où sont vendus les objets fabriqués sur place – l'ensemble représente les traditions vivantes de l'Inde.

Top: View of the temple crafts courtyard with a
ceremonial cart for religious icons.
Bottom: Looking into the temple crafts courtyard.

Oben: Ansicht des Innenhofes mit den Objekten
der Tempelkunst und dem Zeremonienwagen für
die Ikonen.
Unten: Blick in den Innenhof mit der Tempelkunst.

Ci-dessus: Vue de la cour des arts du temple avec
un chariot de cérémonie pour les icônes.
Ci-dessous: Vue de la cour des arts du temple.

The village court with a domed terracotta shrine for
tulsi (basil) plants.

Der Innenhof des Dorfs mit einem kuppelförmigen
Terrakotta-Schrein für die *tulsi* (Basilikum)-Pflanzen.

La cour du village avec un reliquaire en terre cuite
de forme bombée abritant les *tulsi* (basilic).

Top: The entrance facade.

Page 90: At the end of the court is a statue of the god Shiva rising above the pool, which is alimented by a spiral channel sunk into the ground.

Oben: Die Eingangsfassade des Gebäudes.

Seite 90: Im hinteren Teil des Hofes befindet sich eine Statue des Gottes Shiva. Sie ragt über einem Wasserbecken auf, das von einem, im Boden versenkten spiralförmigen Kanal gespeist wird.

Ci-dessus: La façade de l'entrée.

Page 90: Au fond de la cour, se trouve une statue du dieu Shiva placée au-dessus d'un bassin alimenté par un conduit souterrain en spirale.

British Council (1992), New Delhi

The headquarters of the British Council is a set-back, stone-clad cubic structure located on a busy commercial street. The entrance facade is dominated by a gigantic mural by the English painter Howard Hodgkin. The back of the main building abuts a perfectly scaled courtyard defined by two smaller buildings and walls. The vista created along a central axis from the entrance makes transitions from open to closed to open spaces, finally focusing on a statue sitting on a shallow pool of water.

Der Hauptsitz des British Council besteht aus einem zurückgesetzten, mit Steinen verkleideten kubischen Bau, der an einer lebhaften Geschäftsstraße steht. Die Eingangsfassade wird von einem riesigen Wandgemälde des englischen Malers Howard Hodgkin beherrscht. Die Rückseite des Hauptgebäudes grenzt an einen perfekt proportionierten Innenhof, der von zwei kleineren Gebäuden und von Mauern umgrenzt wird. Die Aussicht, die so vom Eingang her über eine zentrale Axe hinweg entsteht, schafft Übergänge zwischen den Räumen. Der Blick verweilt auf einer Statue in einem flachen Wasserbecken.

Le siège du British Council se présente comme une structure cubique, habillée de pierre et construite un peu en retrait dans une rue commerçante animée. Une immense peinture murale du peintre anglais Howard Hodgkin orne la façade de l'entrée. L'arrière du bâtiment principal donne sur une cour de belles proportions délimitée par des murs et deux constructions plus petites. La perspective qui part de l'entrée suit un axe central à travers des espaces ouverts puis fermés puis de nouveau ouverts, s'arrêtant finalement sur une statue posée sur une pièce d'eau peu profonde.

Centre for Astronomy and Astrophysics (1992), Pune

The inter-university Centre seeks to express architecture as a model of the cosmos as manifested in the Vedic *mandala*. The Centre, which pivots around a courtyard like an expanding universe, houses research, office and residential facilities. The building in plan and form juxtaposes rectangular geometry with curvilinear black walls to produce spaces that are quiet and self-contained and others that are dynamic.

In dem inter-universitären Zentrum soll Architektur als ein Modell des Kosmos dargestellt werden, wie es sich im wedischen *mandala* manifestiert. Dieses Zentrum, das sich wie ein sich ausdehnendes Universum um einen Innenhof dreht, beherbergt Forschungs-, Büro- und Wohnräume. Bei dem Gebäude werden rechtwinklige Geometrie und krummlinige Wände gleichermaßen verwandt. Auf diese Weise entstehen Räume, die ruhig und in sich geschlossen sind, während andere wiederum dynamischer wirken.

L'architecture de ce centre interuniversitaire est conçue à la manière du cosmos représenté dans le *mandala* védique. Pivotant autour d'une cour tel un univers en expansion, il abrite les laboratoires de recherche, les bureaux et les résidences. La construction est dans son plan et dans sa forme une juxtaposition de géométrie rectangulaire et de murs noirs curvilignes qui crée une succession d'espaces intimes et sereins et de modules plus ouverts et dynamiques.

The *kund*, or stepped courtyard, in the centre of the complex, surrounded by low building. The figures in the court are of eminent scientists.

Der *kund*, ein mit Stufen versehener Innenhof, im Zentrum des Gebäudekomplexes, umgeben von Flachbauten. Die Statuen im Innenhof stellen bedeutende Wissenschaftler dar.

Le *kund*, une cour en gradins, se trouve au centre du complexe et est entourée de constructions basses. Les statues représentent des scientifiques célèbres.

The interior of the pedestrian entrance pavilion with its domed ceiling and its star-patterned floor evokes notions of the universe.

Das Innere des Eingangspavillons für die Fußgänger, mit seiner kuppelförmigen Decke und dem mit einem Sternmuster versehenen Fußboden, evoziert Vorstellungen des Universums.

A l'intérieur du pavillon de l'entrée piétonne, le plafond en voûte et le sol décoré d'une gigantesque étoile évoquent l'univers.

CSL Associates
Malaysia

Jimmy Lim trained and worked in Australia before returning to practise in Kuala Lumpur in 1974; he established his own firm in 1978. An active member of the profession, serving on various committees both at the architects' institute and for other cultural bodies, he has been concerned with developing an appropriate architectural language for the region. Ranging from residential bungalows to holiday resorts and commercial buildings, his work reflects the indigenous architecture of the region using principles of tropical design and elements such as sloped roofs and naturally ventilated spaces with timber construction. It is often coupled with attention to Chinese *feng-shui*, or geomancy, for the siting and orientation of his buildings. He is perhaps best known for his houses, which he designs with flair, for their overall clarity of expression, attention to detail, and fine crafted quality.

Jimmy Lim hat in Australien gelehrt und gearbeitet, bevor er im Jahre 1974 in Kuala Lumpur die praktische Arbeit wieder aufgenommen und 1978 sein eigenes Unternehmen gegründet hat. Als aktiver Vertreter seines Berufsstandes hat er in verschiedenen Ausschüssen, sowohl am Institut für Architektur wie auch in anderen kulturellen Gremien mitgearbeitet. Sein Interesse ist, eine der Region angemessene Architektursprache zu entwickeln. Angefangen bei Wohnbungalows, über Ferienorte, bis hin zu kommerziellen Bauten, spiegeln seine Arbeiten die einheimische Bauweise dieser Region wider. Er macht sich dabei die Prinzipien des tropischen Baustils zunutze und verwendet Elemente wie Steildächer und naturbelüftete Holzkonstruktionen. In der Plazierung und Ausrichtung seiner Bauten verbindet er dies häufig mit einer Beachtung des chinesischen *feng shui*, der Geomantie. Am bekanntesten ist er vielleicht durch seine Häuser geworden, an denen sich sein Sinn für die Klarheit des Gesamtausdrucks wie auch die Liebe zum Detail und zur handwerklichen Präzision zeigt.

Jimmy Lim a étudié et travaillé en Australie, puis est revenu exercer à Kuala Lumpur en 1974 et a fondé son propre bureau en 1978. Personnalité très active de l'architecture, membre de plusieurs comités dont celui de l'Institut d'architecture et d'autres institutions culturelles, il a voulu élaborer un langage architectural adapté à la région. Comprenant aussi bien des bungalows résidentiels que des lieux de villégiature et des réalisations commerciales, son œuvre reflète l'architecture autochtone en reprenant des éléments de cette région tropicale tels que les toits en pente et les espaces aérés naturellement des constructions en bois. On y remarque souvent un intérêt pour le *feng-shui* chinois, ou géomancie, pour le choix du site et l'orientation du bâtiment. C'est peut-être pour ses maisons qu'il est le mieux connu: elles révèlent une grande rigueur ainsi qu'une attention particulière au détail et à la qualité.

Salinger House (1992), south of Kuala Lumpur, typical of Lim's work, uses the pavilion concept.

Das Salinger Haus (1992), im Süden von Kuala Lumpur, ist typisch für Lims Werk; es greift das Pavillon-Konzept auf.

Salinger House (1992) au sud de Kuala Lumpur, typique de l'œuvre de Lim; elle reprend le concept du pavillon.

Modular Timber Mosques
(1985 and ongoing), Pahang

Based on the traditional rural Malay mosque with its central space and pyramidal tiered roofs, the architect developed a design for a repeatable building type. The client, the institution for timber resources for the State of Pahang, Malaysia, insisted that timber and a "Pahang theme" had to be used. Jimmy Lim designed five similar types of mosques based on a 2.5 metre (approximately 8 feet) square module, raised on stilts, varying in size to accommodate between 300 and 600 worshipers, and with two- to three-tiered roofs. 33 such mosques have been built in different site conditions, and they seem to have succeeded in meeting the people's cultural aspirations.

Ausgehend von der traditionell ländlichen malaiischen Moschee mit ihrem zentralen Innenraum und den pyramidenförmig abgestuften Dächern, hat der Architekt einen Entwurf für einen Prototyp dieser Bauart entwickelt. Der Auftraggeber, das Institut für Holzressourcen des Staates Pahang, Malaysia, bestand darauf, daß Holz sowie ein »Pahang-Thema« zu verwenden sei. Lim entwarf fünf sich ähnelnde Moscheen, die auf einem 2,5 m großen, quadratischen Bauelement (Modul) beruhen, das auf Pfeilern errichtet wird, für 300 bis 600 Gläubige gedacht ist und zwei- bis dreistufige Dächer aufweist. 33 solcher Moscheen sind auf jeweils unterschiedlich beschaffenem Gelände errichtet worden, und es ist gelungen, den kulturellen Wünschen der Menschen zu entsprechen.

Jimmy Lim s'est inspiré de la mosquée rurale malaisienne, avec sa cour centrale et ses toits pyramidaux étagés, pour concevoir son projet modulable. Le client, l'administration des ressources en bois de l'Etat de Pahang, exigea l'emploi du bois et un «thème de Pahang» traditionnel. Jimmy Lim a dessiné cinq types de mosquées similaires basées sur un module carré de 2,5 m de côté posé sur pilotis; elles peuvent accueillir entre 300 et 600 fidèles selon les dimensions et ont un toit à deux ou trois sections superposées. Trente-trois de ces mosquées ont été édifiées dans différents sites. Elles semblent répondre aux aspirations culturelles de la population.

Page 96: Main entrance façade of a mosque with additional ancillary pavilions. The use of painted, galvanized metal sheeting for the roof was controversial in the beginning but won acceptance quickly.

Seite 96: Vorderseite mit dem Haupteingang der Moschee und weiteren Nebenpavillons. Die Verwendung eines galvanisierten, mit Anstrich versehenen Blechs für das Dach war anfangs umstritten, fand aber binnen kurzer Zeit doch Beifall.

Page 96: Façade de l'entrée principale avec les pavillons annexes. Le toit en feuilles de métal galvanisé peint très controversé au début, est aujourd'hui bien accepté.

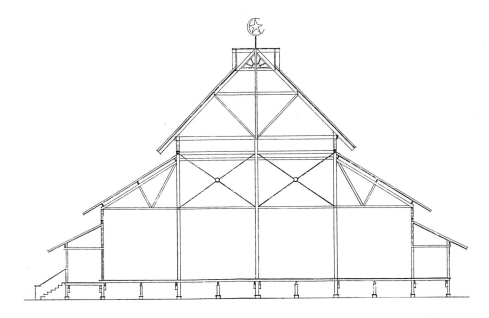

Bottom: Interior of the mosque during prayers. The exposed timber structure forms part of the simple aesthetic of the design.

Unten: Innenraum der Moschee während der Gebete. Die unverkleidete Holzkonstruktion macht einen Teil der schlichten Ästhetik dieses Entwurfs aus.

Ci-dessous: L'intérieur de la mosquée pendant la prière. La charpente apparente s'inscrit dans l'esthétique très simple du bâtiment.

Top: Section through a typical two-tiered roof mosque.

Oben: Schnitt einer typischen Moschee mit dem zweistufigen Dach.

Ci-dessus: Coupe transversale d'une mosquée-type à toits étagés.

The living area on the first level consists of a double-height space with the master bedroom mezzanine level at the top.

Der auf der ersten Etage gelegene Wohnbereich besteht aus einem Raum von doppelter Höhe; oben die Zwischengeschoßebene mit den Hauptschlaf-zimmern.

Le salon qui se trouve au premier niveau se pré-sente comme un espace à double hauteur; la partie supérieure est une mezzanine aménagée en cham-bre à coucher.

The covered ground floor area is used as an entrance and informal entertainment space.

Die überdachte Erdgeschoßfläche dient sowohl als Eingangsbereich wie auch als Raum für Ge-selligkeiten.

Le rez-de-chaussée couvert sert d'entrée et d'espace convivial.

Schnyder House
(1986–92), Kuala Lumpur

Located in Bangsar, a suburb of Kuala Lumpur, the house sits atop a hill overlooking the city. The regional vernacular, with its pavilion structures, overhanging roofs, and timber stilt construction, is used to good effect. The semi-circular house pavilion has a large swimming pool and covered entertainment area with a living level above and a bedroom suite at the top. An addition of two guest suites is built into the hill below the house.

In Bangsar, einem Vorort von Kuala Lumpur, liegt dieses Haus hoch oben auf einem Hügel, von dem aus man die gesamte Stadt überblickt. Die für die Region typische Bauweise mit ihren Pavillons, ihren vorstehenden Dächern und ihren Holzpfahlbauten, wird hier wirkungsvoll eingesetzt. Der halbkreisförmige Hauspavillon hat einen großen Swimmingpool und einen überdachten Bereich für die Freizeitaktivitäten, darüber liegen die Wohnräume, und ganz oben befindet sich die Suite mit den Schlafzimmern. Zwei weitere Suiten mit Gästezimmern sind in den Hügel unterhalb des Hauses eingebaut.

Située à Bangsar, dans la banlieue de Kuala Lumpur, la maison se trouve au sommet d'une colline dominant la ville. L'architecte a su se servir de l'architecture vernaculaire avec ses structures pavillonnaires, ses toits en surplomb et ses constructions en bois sur pilotis. Le pavillon semi-circulaire abrite une grande piscine, un espace de détente et de réception, un séjour au premier niveau et une chambre à coucher tout en haut. Deux appartements d'hôtes ont été construits dans la colline en dessous de la maison.

Nayyar Ali **Dada** & Associates
Pakistan

Nayyar Ali Dada, whose first passion was painting, is a well-known Pakistani architect based in Lahore, where most of his work is located. Education, architectural issues related to context, history, and the culture of Islam are among his prominent concerns. He bemoans the profession's lack of purpose, advocating that architecture be "an extraordinary mixture of the pragmatic and spiritual." A thoughtful person, he is best known for the quality of his designs. First known for his houses for upper-income families, he is now better known for institutional and cultural buildings. He uses brick and concrete in his works, which reflect the modernist vein in architecture, but he consciously injects new interpretations of local idioms into them. Dada's more recent works reveal a concern with the environment around them, with energy efficiency, and their users' reactions, a all of which he believes are good Islamic and humanistic values.

Nayyar Ali Dada, der zunächst ein passionierter Maler war, ist heute ein bekannter pakistanischer Architekt mit Sitz in Lahore, wo auch der größte Teil seiner Bauten steht. Er befaßt sich vor allem mit Fragen der Bildung, mit Problemen einer kontextbezogenen Architektur sowie mit der Geschichte und Kultur des Islam und beklagt die mangelnden Ziel- und Zweckvorstellungen seines Berufsstandes. Für ihn muß Architektur »eine außergewöhnliche Mischung aus Pragmatischem und Geistigem« sein. Anfangs machte er sich einen Namen mit Einfamilienhäusern für den gehobenen Einkommensbereich. Inzwischen ist er durch seine öffentlichen und kulturellen Bauten noch bekannter geworden. Er arbeitet mit Ziegelstein und Beton, Materialien, die die modernistische Strömung in der Architektur widerspiegeln, läßt aber bewußt auch ganz neue Interpretationen des lokalen Idioms mit einfließen. An kürzlich entstandenen Bauten zeigt sich sein Interesse an der Umgebung, an der effizienten Nutzung von Energien und an den Reaktionen der Bewohner – Dinge, die in seinen Augen gute alte islamische und humanistische Werte darstellen.

Nayyar Ali Dada dont la première passion fut la peinture – travaille à Lahore où se trouvent d'ailleurs la plupart de ses réalisations. Cet architecte célèbre s'intéresse à l'enseignement et à l'architecture dans le contexte de l'islam, et déplore le manque de desseins de la profession, alors que, dit-il, l'architecture devrait être «une extraordinaire fusion du pragmatique et du spirituel». Cet homme réfléchi est connu pour l'impeccable qualité de ses plans. Il s'est fait d'abord remarquer par ses maisons bourgeoises, mais c'est à ses édifices institutionnels et culturels qu'il doit sa véritable notoriété. Il utilise la brique et le béton, tout en introduisant sciemment dans ses œuvres des idiomes locaux qu'il a interprétés. Les derniers projets d'Ali Dada révèlent une véritable préoccupation pour l'environnement, l'utilisation minimale de l'énergie et les réactions des utilisateurs – indiscutablement pour lui de vraies valeurs islamiques et humanistes.

Detail of the main entrance of the Open-Air Theatre (1990) in Lahore, illustrating the architect's characteristic use of brick enlivened by blue tilework.

Detail des Haupteinganges des Freilichttheaters (1990) in Lahore. Hier zeigt sich die Vorliebe des Architekten für ein mit blauen Kacheln durchsetztes Mauerwerk.

Détail de l'entrée principale du théâtre en plein air de Lahore (1990). On remarque la prédilection de l'architecte pour la brique rehaussée de carreaux de faïence bleus.

Top left: The foyer of the main auditorium expresses the structure clearly.
Top right: Staircase in the art gallery.
Right: Site plan.

Oben links: In dem Foyer des Hauptauditoriums kommt die Konstruktion voll zur Geltung.
Oben rechts: Treppenaufgang innerhalb der Kunstgalerie.
Rechts: Lageplan.

Ci-dessus à gauche: Le foyer de la salle principale est révélateur de l'ensemble de la structure.
Ci-dessus à droite: Volée d'escalier dans la galerie d'art.
A droite: Plan de situation.

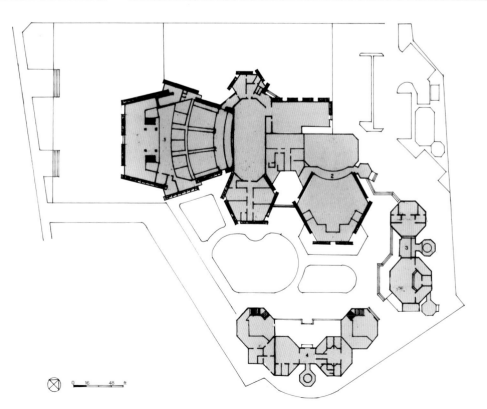

0   16   48   ft

Alhamra Art Centre (1976–87), Lahore

Built in phases over a decade, the arts centre located in the heart of the city contains three auditoriums, a gallery, classrooms, a library, office space, and a recording studio. Monumental in scale, it is reminiscent of the region's citadel architecture. Essentially polygonal in plan to accommodate the auditoriums, the stark simplicity of the brick-clad complex is striking. There is also an open-air theatre-in-the-round (1990) that extends the use of the external spaces.

The main auditorium (Hall 1) from the road. The monumental sloping brick walls stand as guardians to this citadel of culture and make its presence felt in the cityscape.

In insgesamt 10 Jahren erbaut, bietet dieses im Herzen der Stadt liegende Kunstzentrum Räumlichkeiten für drei Hörsäle, eine Galerie, Klassenräume, eine Bibliothek, Büros und ein Aufnahmestudio. In seinen monumentalen Ausmaßen erinnert es an die Zitadellen-Architektur dieser Region. Der mit Ziegelstein verkleidete Komplex beruht, zur Unterbringung der Hörsäle, auf einem im wesentlichen polygonalen Grundriß. Ein kreisförmig angelegtes Freilichttheater (1990) erweitert die Nutzung der Außenräume.

Das Hauptauditorium (Halle 1), von der Straße aus gesehen. Die monumentalen, schräg gestellten Backsteinmauern stehen wie Torhüter vor dieser Zitadelle der Kultur und machen sich im Stadtbild spürbar bemerkbar.

La construction de ce centre au cœur de la ville s'est effectuée en plusieurs phases durant une décennie. Il comprend trois auditoriums, une galerie, des classes, une bibliothèque, des bureaux et un studio d'enregistrement. De par sa monumentalité, il évoque l'architecture fortifiée de la région. De forme polygonale pour y abriter les auditoriums, cet édifice en brique frappe par sa simplicité absolue. Un théâtre en plein air (1990) permet une plus large utilisation des espaces extérieurs.

La salle principale (Hall 1) vue de la rue. Inclinés, monumentaux, les murs en brique sont les gardiens de cette citadelle de la culture et s'imposent dans le paysage urbain par leur forte présence.

Punjab House (1991), Islamabad

Set against the picturesque Margalla Hills on a high sloping site above the city, the building is a residence for senior government officials visiting the capital from the Punjab state. Axially and symmetrically organized, the blocks surround landscaped courtyards and draw upon 17th-century Mughal buildings for inspiration. The bedrooms, all with striking views, are clustered around 3-storey atriums finished in marble.

In den pittoresken Margalla Hills, oberhalb der Stadt fungiert das Gebäude als Residenz für höhere Regierungsbeamte, die der Hauptstadt einen Besuch abstatten. Die Wohnblöcke sind achsensymmetrisch um die landschaftlich ausgestalteten Innenhöfe angelegt und von den Mughal-Bauten des siebzehnten Jahrhunderts inspiriert. Die Schlafzimmer, die durchweg eine phantastische Aussicht bieten, gruppieren sich jeweils um die dreigeschossigen, mit Marmor ausgekleideten Innenhöfe.

Bâtie sur un site en pente dans les pittoresques Margalla Hills, cette construction est une résidence pour les hauts fonctionnaires en visite dans la capitale de l'Etat du Punjab. Organisés de façon symétrique et axiale, les différents bâtiments sont disposés autour de cours aménagées et s'inspirent des constructions mogholes du XVIIe siècle. Les chambres, toutes dotées de vues magnifiques, sont réparties autour de l'atrium de trois étages habillé de marbre.

The complex seen from the main road. While the complex uses a contemporary idiom, the solid geometric shapes and porticoes recall the Mughal buildings of the Punjab.

Der Gebäudekomplex, von der Hauptstraße aus gesehen. Der Komplex verwendet insgesamt eine zeitgenössische Architektursprache; die soliden geometrischen Formen und Säulengänge erinnern dagegen an die Mughal-Bauten des Punjab.

Vue perspective du complexe depuis la rue principale. Si l'idiome de cette réalisation est contemporain, les portiques et les formes solides, géométriques rappellent, eux, les constructions mogholes du Punjab.

The covered walkway around the courtyard offers a magnificent view of the Margalla Hills beyond.

Der um den Innerhof herumführende, überdachte Wandelgang bietet eine phantastische Aussicht auf die im Hintergrund liegenden Margalla-Hügel.

La galerie autour de la cour intérieure offre une vue splendide sur les collines de Margalla.

The main foyer and sitting area of the central building with its patterned marble floor is overlooked by the balconies leading to the bedrooms.

Blick von den zu den Schlafräumen führenden Galerien auf das zentrale Foyer und den Sitzbereich des Hauptgebäudes mit seinem gemusterten Marmorboden.

Des galeries conduisant aux chambres surplombent le grand foyer aménagé en salon et agrémenté d'un sol en marbre à motifs.

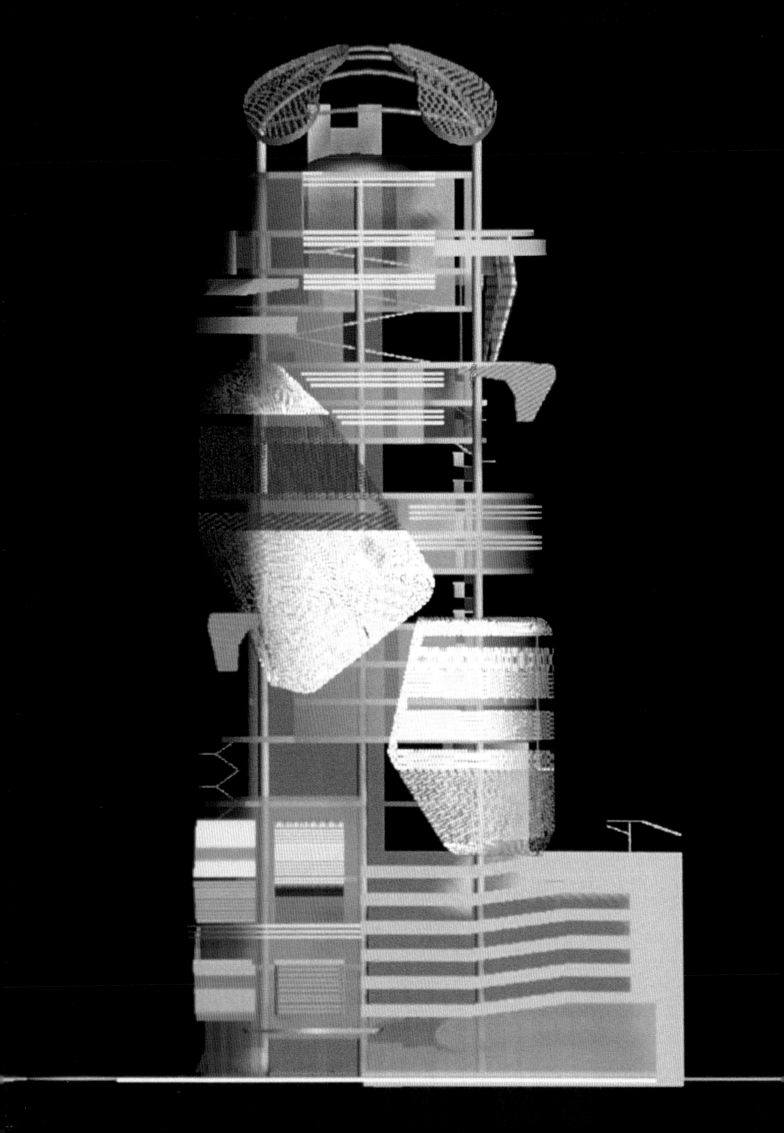

T.R. **Hamzah** & **Yeang**
Malaysia

Ken Yeang

Robert Hamzah

The project for Hitechniaga Tower (1994) in Kuala Lumpur in which climatic design and high-tech elements are interpreted within and around a skeletal frame.

Das Projekt des Hitechniaga Tower (1994) in Kuala Lumpur bei dem Klimatisierung und High-Tech-Elemente in einen Skelettrahmen einbezogen sind.

Le projet de réalisation de la tour Hitechniaga (1994) à Kuala Lumpur, dont l'ossature légère intègre contraintes climatiques et éléments high tech.

Ken Yeang is a well-known contributor to the international architectural discourse as a proponent of a regionalist approach to design. He has been in private practise in Malaysia since 1976 with Tengku Robert Hamzah, specializing in high-rise building and low-energy design. Both were trained in the UK and are of Chinese and Malay descent, respectively, an effective partnership in Malaysia. Yeang favours a design approach that takes into account the architectural and natural characteristics of a region, particularly its climate and ecology, by employing contemporary technology. He is particularly noted for his innovative design of roof and filter systems for climate control and energy, and the use of "gardens in the air" in his high-rise buildings, which represent some of the firm's best work. He takes an active role as a theoretician internationally through teaching, lecturing, and writing on architectural and urban issues relating to Southeast Asia. The firm continues to be experimental.

Ken Yeang ist ein bekannter und aktiver Vertreter des internationalen Architektur-Diskurses und Befürworter eines regionalistisch geprägten Designs. Seit 1976 war er, zusammen mit Tengku Robert Hamzah, in Malaysia tätig, wo er sich auf den Bau von Hochhäusern und energiesparendes Design spezialisiert hat. Beide erhielten ihre Ausbildung in Großbritannien und sind chinesischer bzw. malaiischer Abstammung, was in Malaysia eine effiziente Partnerschaft darstellt. Yeang favorisiert ein Design, das den architektonischen und natürlichen Gegebenheiten einer Region durch die Anwendung zeitgemäßer Technologien Rechnung trägt, insbesondere dem Klima und der Ökologie. Besondere Beachtung finden seine innovativen Entwürfe für Dächer und Filteranlagen zur Klimaregelung und Energiekontrolle sowie die in seine Hochhausbauten integrierten »Freiluftgärten«, die zu den besten Arbeiten dieser Gruppe gehören. Durch seine Lehrveranstaltungen, Vorlesungen und Veröffentlichungen zu Fragen der Architektur und Stadtplanung im Raum Südostasien kommt ihm als Theoretiker international eine aktive Rolle zu. Die Gruppe arbeitet weiterhin experimentell.

Le discours architectural international doit beaucoup à Ken Yeang et à sa prise de position en faveur de l'approche régionaliste en architecture. Il dirige sa propre agence en Malaisie depuis 1976 conjointement avec Tengku Robert Hamzah et s'est spécialisé dans la construction de gratte-ciel économes en énergie. Respectivement d'origine chinoise et malaise, Yeang et Hamzah ont été formés en Grande-Bretagne et ils se complètent fort bien. Yeang prône la prise en compte des particularités architecturales et naturelles de la région, en particulier son climat et son écologie, grâce aux technologies modernes. Il est réputé pour ses ingénieux systèmes de toits et de filtres qui servent à contrôler le climat et l'énergie, et pour les «jardins suspendus» de ses gratte-ciel qui comptent parmi les plus belles réussites de l'agence. Son rôle de théoricien est international car il enseigne, donne des conférences, et publie des études sur l'architecture et l'urbanisme dans le Sud-Est asiatique. L'agence poursuit son travail de recherche.

Roof Roof House
(1984), Selangor, Kuala Lumpur

The house designed as Yeang's own residence shaped the building's enclosure as an "environmental filter." Its north-south orientation protects the main spaces from the sun and takes advantage of the prevailing southwest winds. The roofs are covered with a louvered umbrella roof that shades the whole building – giving rise to the name of the house. The pool also acts as a climate regulator. The design is contemporary and constitutes an innovative response to place and lifestyle.

Bei dem Entwurf für sein eigenes Wohnhaus hat Yeang dem äußeren Rahmen des Bauwerks die Gestalt eines »Umweltfilters« gegeben. Seine Nord-Süd-Ausrichtung schützt die wichtigsten Räume vor der Sonne und macht sich die dort meist herrschenden Südwestwinde zunutze. Über den Einzeldächern befindet sich nochmals ein gekrümmtes Schirmdach, das dem gesamten Gebäude Schatten spendet – was dem Haus auch seinen Namen gegeben hat. Das Wasserbecken dient gleichzeitig der Klimaregelung. Das Design ist zeitgemäß und korrespondiert auf innovative Weise mit dem Ort und der dortigen Lebensweise.

Dans cette maison conçue pour être la résidence personnelle de Yeang, l'enveloppe sert de «filtre environnemental». Son orientation nord-sud protège les espaces principaux du soleil et profite des vents dominants du sud-ouest. Les toits sont recouverts d'un toit parasol à claire-voie qui donne de l'ombre à l'ensemble, d'où le nom de la maison (maison toit sur toit). Le bassin agit aussi comme régulateur du climat. Le dessin est contemporain et constitue une réponse novatrice au lieu et au mode de vie.

Section through the 2-storey house roof terrace and pool.

Schnitt des zweistöckigen Hauses, des Dachs, der Terrasse und des Pools.

Vue en coupe de la maison, avec sa terrasse et son bassin.

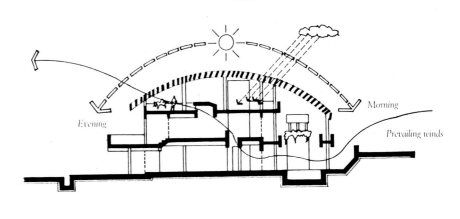

Page 108 + 109 bottom: The curvilinear concrete louvered shade as a second roof unites the fragmented composition of the masses under it.

Seite 108 + 109 unten: Das gekrümmte Betonschirmdach macht, als ein zweites Dach, die fragmentierte Komposition der unter ihm liegenden Baukörper zu einer Einheit.

Page 108 + 109 ci-dessous: Le brise-soleil curviligne en béton, qui fait aussi office de second toit, unit les masses morcelées placées sous lui.

Menara Mesiniaga
(1992), Selangor, Kuala Lumpur

One of the most interesting high-rise buildings in Asia, Menara Mesiniaga (*Mesiniaga* means "business machine") brings together several innovative features. The vertical planting is introduced in the north facade and spirals down the building by means of "skycourts", or terraces. External louvers are used as sun shades, and the north and south facades, which do not receive direct sunlight, have curtain-wall glazing.

In einem der interessantesten Hochhausbauten Asiens, der Menara Mesiniaga (*Mesiniaga* bedeutet »Geschäftsmaschine«) sind gleich mehrere innovative Züge miteinander verbunden worden. Die vertikal angelegte Bepflanzung beginnt an der Nordfassade und wird spiralförmig, über »Lichthöfe« oder Terrassen, an dem Gebäude heruntergeführt. Die außen angebrachten Belüftungsklappen fungieren als Markisen, und die Nord- und Südfassaden, auf die kein direktes Sonnenlicht fällt, sind mit einer Blendwandverglasung versehen.

Menara Mesiniaga (*Mesiniaga* signifie «machine commerciale») est l'un des buildings les plus intéressants d'Asie car il comporte plusieurs innovations. Cette construction se présente sous la forme de spirales montées sur des supports verticaux créant sur la façade nord des terrasses ou «cours aériennes». Des brise-soleil extérieurs protègent des ardeurs du soleil et les façades nord et sud qui n'ont pas d'ensoleillement direct sont revêtues d'un mur-rideau en verre.

The generous high-tech foyer continues inside the external building vocabulary.

In dem großzügig angelegten High-Tech Foyer setzt sich das Architekturvokabular des Äußeren fort.

La spacieuse entrée «high-tech» reprend le vocabulaire architectural de l'extérieur de la tour.

Page 111: The 14-storey building with its gleaming metallic skin and spiraling terraces projects 21st-century imagery.

Seite 111: Der 14-geschossige Bau mit seiner glänzenden, metallischen »Haut« und den spiralförmig verlaufenden Terrassen stellt eine Projektion der Bildsprache des 21. Jahrhunderts dar.

Page 111: Cette tour de 14 étages projette une image du XXIe siècle avec sa membrane métallique miroitante et ses terrasses en spirale.

Kwang-Jang Architects
South Korea

Kim Won, principal of Kwang-Jang (or Architects' Group Forum), formed his own firm in 1976. He came to prominence upon winning the competition for the Korean Exhibition Centre in 1977. Rooted in the Modern Movement, Kim's buildings make powerful statements in the landscape. Some of his work is tempered by the use of brick and careful detailing, whilst others using stone and concrete are brutal in their appearance. Known for its institutional buildings, the firm has won numerous competitions and honours from the Korea Institute of Architects. Kim is also an urban designer, a prominent member of various boards and foundations, and a strong advocate for architecture to express a modern Korean identity. A multifaceted individual, his work, amongst the best in the country, continues to grow and change within his chosen idiom.

Kim Won, der Chef der Kwang-Jang Gruppe (bzw. Architects' Group Forum) eröffnete im Jahre 1976 sein eigenes Büro. Er machte von sich reden, als er 1977 den Wettbewerb für das Korean Exhibition Centre gewann. Kims Bauwerke, die in der Moderne wurzeln, sind machtvolle Darstellungen in der Landschaft. Ein Teil seiner Arbeiten wird durch die Verwendung von Backstein und die sorgfältige Ausgestaltung der Details etwas gemäßigt, andere, bei denen er Stein und Beton verwendet, wirken dagegen ungeheuer massiv. Die Gruppe ist ursprünglich durch ihre Verwaltungsbauten bekannt geworden, sie hat zahlreiche Wettbewerbe gewonnen und erhielt Auszeichnungen vom Korea Institute of Architects. Kim ist gleichzeitig Stadtplaner; er ist ferner ein prominentes Mitglied in verschiedenen Ausschüssen und Stiftungen sowie strikter Befürworter einer Architektur, in der eine moderne koreanische Identität zum Ausdruck kommt. Er ist eine facettenreiche Persönlichkeit, und seine Arbeiten, die zu den besten des Landes gehören, wachsen und verändern sich weiterhin innerhalb des von ihm selbst gewählten Idioms.

Kim Won, directeur de Kwan-Jang, créa sa propre agence en 1976. Il se fit connaître en remportant le concours du Centre coréen des expositions en 1977. Enracinées dans le Mouvement moderne, ses réalisations sont puissamment expressives dans le paysage. L'emploi de la brique et le grand soin accordé aux détails tempèrent certaines constructions, d'autres, réalisées en pierre et en béton, ont un aspect plus brutal. Célèbre pour ses édifices institutionnels, l'agence a remporté de nombreux concours et a été honorée plusieurs fois par l'Institut coréen des architectes. Kim est de surcroît urbaniste. Il est membre de plusieurs conseils d'administration et fondations et milite en faveur d'une architecture exprimant l'identité coréenne moderne. Personnalité aux multiples facettes, l'architecte a à son actif une œuvre – une des meilleures du pays – qui continue à croître et évoluer à l'intérieur de l'idiome qu'il a choisi.

The simple round windows set in the brickwork of the Convent of St. Paul de Chartres (1983) in Seoul.

Die Fassade des Klosters St. Paul de Chartres (1983), in Seoul, wird durch schlichte runde Fenster durchbrochen.

La façade en brique du Couvent Saint-Paul-de-Chartres à Séoul (1983) est percée de fenêtres circulaires d'une grande sobriété.

Gallery Bing
(1985–90), Seoul

This art gallery stands out as a sculptural object in a dense urban environment – an image of an ice crystal – functioning as a focal point along the road. Modern in its imagery and construction, a space-frame structure with aluminium panels, this 950-square-metre space provides an exemplary setting for modern works of art.

Diese Galerie fällt ins Auge als ein skulpturales Objekt in einem dicht besiedelten Stadtgebiet – ein Bild von einem Eiskristall – das für die ganze Straße eine Art Blickfang darstellt. Dieser 950 Quadratmeter umfassende Raum gibt durch seine moderne Bildsprache und Konstruktion mit Aluminium-Verkleidung einen geradezu beispielhaften Rahmen für moderne Kunstwerke ab.

La galerie d'art est un objet sculptural qui tranche sur un environnement urbain compact. Ressemblant à un cristal de glace, il est le point de mire dans la rue où il est situé. Moderne de par son expression et sa construction et conçue comme une ossature en panneaux d'aluminium, cette galerie abritant 950 m² de surface d'exposition est un cadre parfait pour des œuvres d'art modernes.

The space-frame enclosure creates a single flexible space in the interior.

Die Konstruktion läßt im Inneren einen einzigen, flexiblen Raum entstehen.

L'intérieur de la galerie se présente comme un espace d'un seul tenant et d'une grande souplesse.

Page 114: View of the gallery from the street.

Seite 114: Blick von der Straße auf die Galerie.

Page 114: Vue de la galerie depuis la rue.

The Sisters' Convent of Korean Martyrs (1993), Seoul

The project was designed to complement and extend an existing building in a dense urban area. It consists of a chapel and cloisters, dining rooms, bedrooms, and a library, on five floors. Built of cement-concrete with red brick facing and copper-plate roofing, the major addition has open courtyards around which the buildings are staggered to achieve an orientation allowing natural lighting and ventilation.

Das Projekt wurde zur Ergänzung und Erweiterung eines bereits vorhandenen Gebäudes entworfen und liegt in einem dicht besiedelten Stadtgebiet. Es besteht aus einer Kapelle und Kreuzgängen, Speisesälen, Schlafräumen und einer Bibliothek auf insgesamt fünf Stockwerken. Der Hauptanbau besteht aus Zementbeton, der mit rotem Backstein verkleidet und mit einer Kupferblech-Bedachung versehen wurde. Er hat offene Innenhöfe, um die herum die einzelnen Bauten leicht versetzt angeordnet sind, so daß für alle Gebäude eine natürliche Beleuchtung und Belüftung gewährleistet ist.

Le projet avait pour but de compléter et d'agrandir un édifice plus ancien situé dans une zone urbaine très dense. Le couvent de sœurs, d'une hauteur de cinq étages, comprend une chapelle, des cloîtres, des réfectoires, des chambres et une bibliothèque. Le principal ajout est construit en béton et en ciment avec un revêtement de brique, son toit est en cuivre. Le complexe comprend plusieurs cours ouvertes autour desquelles les bâtiments sont arrangés de manière à laisser pénétrer la lumière et l'air.

The stark white space of the brightlyl lit interior of the chapel is complemented by the light wood paneling.

Das kahle Weiß des hell erleuchteten Innenraums der Kapelle wird durch die helle Holzvertäfelung noch vervollkommnet.

L'intérieur de la chapelle est un sobre espace blanc plein de lumière, rehaussé par des boiseries claires.

Page 117: The powerful and simple juxtaposition of forms gives the complex a serene elegance.

Seite 117: Das kraftvolle und einfache Nebeneinander der Formen verleiht dem Gebäudekomplex eine schlichte Eleganz.

Page 117: Simple et puissante, la juxtaposition des formes donne à cette réalisation une élégance tranquille.

William **Lim** Associates
Singapore

William Lim

Mok Wei Wei

Unit 8 (1984), sometimes known as the "pink apartment building" tries to synthesize post-modern and regional building concerns.

Unit 8 (1984), auch »das pinkfarbige Hochhaus« genannt, vereint post-moderne und regionale Bauaspekte.

L'Unité 8 (1984) parfois appelée «l'immeuble rose» s'efforce de concilier post-modernisme et esprit régional.

William Lim has exerted considerable influence on architecture and urban planning in South-east Asia. He began practising first in Kuala Lumpur in 1960, working in a modernist idiom, and concentrating on residential and commercial works. Lim moved to Singapore to start a much larger firm, Design Partnership, in 1967, which built innovatory large-scale shopping complexes on which much subsequent commercial development in the city was modelled. During the 1980s he worked on projects related to conservation and revitalization, and experimented briefly with post-modernist ideas whilst setting up a new practise, William Lim Associates, with a group of younger designers and a partner, Mok Wei Wei, in 1986. With its studio-like atmosphere, the firm remains small, and its projects pay particular attention to improving the urban environment and exploring themes of Southeast Asian tradition and identity. Lim has written extensively on the city and urbanization in South-east Asia. His work continues to evolve in a lively dialogue with current architectural theories, stimulated by emphasis on group working methods to generate creativity.

William Lim hat auf die Architektur und Stadtplanung Südostasiens einen beachtlichen Einfluß ausgeübt. 1960 hat er in Kuala Lumpur seine ersten Bauten errichtet, wobei er einen modernistischen Stil verwendete und sich auf Wohnhäuser und kommerzielle Bauten konzentrierte. Lim zog dann nach Singapur, wo er 1967 ein größeres Unternehmen gründete, die Design Partnership, die groß angelegte Einkaufszentren baute. Während der achtziger Jahre arbeitete Lim an Projekten, die auf Erhaltung und Neubelebung abzielten und experimentierte für kurze Zeit auch mit postmodernen Ideen, als er 1986, zusammen mit einer Gruppe jüngerer Designer und einem Partner, Mok Wei Wei, ein neues Büro unter dem Namen William Lim Associates eröffnete. Mit seiner studio-ähnlichen Atmosphäre bleibt das Unternehmen klein, und seine Projekte befassen sich insbesondere mit der Verbesserung der städtischen Umwelt und dem Studium südostasiatischer Tradition und Identität. Lim hat umfangreiche Schriften zum Thema Stadt und Verstädterung in Südostasien verfaßt. Zur Förderung der Kreativität legt er sehr viel Wert auf Teamarbeit.

William Lim a exercé une influence considérable sur l'architecture et l'urbanisme de l'Asie du Sud-Est. Sa carrière commence à Kuala Lumpur en 1960. Son idiome architectural est alors moderne et il travaille essentiellement sur des projets résidentiels et commerciaux. Lim s'installe ensuite à Singapour pour y ouvrir en 1967 une agence nettement plus grande, la Design Partnership. Il construit de grands centres commerciaux qui serviront de modèles pour le développement commercial de la ville. Dans les années 80, Lim travaille sur des projets de sauvegarde et de réhabilitation urbaines et s'essaie au postmodernisme. En 1986, il ouvre un nouveau bureau d'architectes, le William Lim Associates, avec Mok Wei Wei et un groupe de jeunes collaborateurs. Il s'intéresse alors beaucoup à l'amélioration de l'environnement urbain et explore des thèmes traditionnels et identitaires du Sud-Est asiatique. Lim a beaucoup écrit sur la ville et l'urbanisation de cette région. Il continue à évoluer dans un dialogue vivant avec les théories architecturales actuelles et avec son équipe.

Central Square
(1990), Kuala Lumpur

This urban shopping complex is adjacent to Kuala Lumpur's Central Market (also co-designed by Lim). The building is divided into two sections and is further broken down into a series of smaller blocks, reminiscent of the local shop-houses in scale. The brightly coloured buildings and their curvilinear forms draw inspiration from the post-modernist idiom, creating an eclectic and lively environment.

Dieses städtische Einkaufszentrum grenzt an den Central Market von Kuala Lumpur, (bei dessen Entwurf Lim ebenfalls mitgewirkt hat). Der Bau besteht aus zwei Abschnitten und ist nochmals in eine Reihe kleinerer Blöcke untergliedert, die in ihrer Größe an die ortsüblichen, kleinen Läden erinnern. Die in leuchtenden Farben gehaltenen Gebäude mit ihren krummlinigen Formen sind vom postmodernen Idiom inspiriert und schaffen ein ebenso eklektizistisches wie lebhaftes Ambiente.

Ce centre commercial est adjacent au Central Market de Kuala Lumpur (une co-création de Lim). Le bâtiment se divise en deux sections puis se décompose en une série de petits blocs qui par leurs dimensions rappellent les maisons échoppes locales. Les couleurs vives et les formes curvilignes, d'inspiration postmoderne, créent un environnement éclectique et vivant.

Upper-level cafe overlooking the pedestrian mall.

Café im Obergeschoß mit Blick auf die Fußgängerzone.

Le café-restaurant situé au niveau supérieur donne sur la zone piétonne.

The building viewed from the main square with the pedestrian mall to the right.

Das Gebäude vom Hauptplatz aus gesehen, mit der Fußgängerzone auf der rechten Seite.

Le centre vu depuis la place principale, avec la zone piétonne sur la droite.

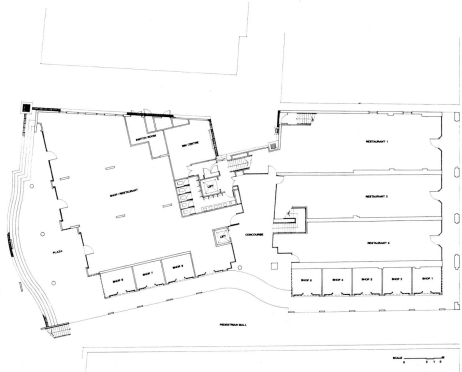

Ground-level plan.

Grundriß des Erdgeschosses.

Plan du rez-de-chaussée.

Boon House
(1994), Singapore

The Boon House deconstructs and expresses the different elements of the accommodations separately as two pavilions and an elongated block surrounded by small gardens. Built for entertaining, the house expresses its functions, structure, and use of materials with clarity and a playful elegance.

Das Boon House dekonstruiert die verschiedenen Wohnbauelemente und bringt sie in Form von zwei Pavillons und einem langgestreckten Bau, umgeben von kleinen Gärten, jeweils gesondert zum Ausdruck. Das Haus wurde für gesellige Anlässe gebaut, und drückt in seinen Funktionen, seiner Bauweise und in der Verwendung seiner Materialien eine klare, spielerische Eleganz aus.

La Maison Boon décompose et exprime à la fois les différents éléments de l'habitation en deux pavillons et une structure de forme allongée entourés de petits jardins. Construite pour recevoir, la maison exprime ses fonctions, sa structure et l'emploi des matériaux avec clarté et une élégance ludique.

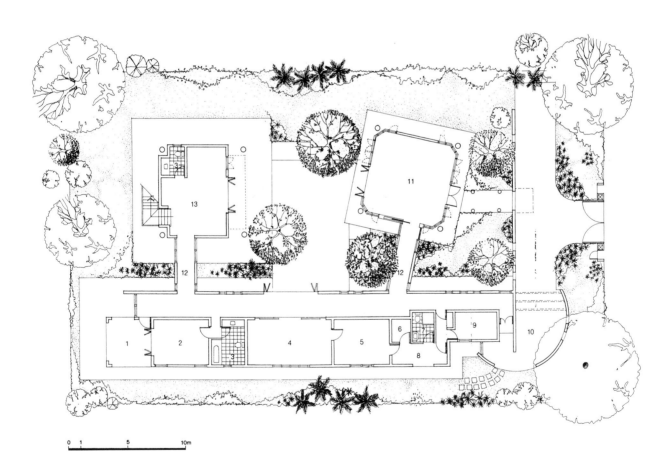

0 1   5   10m

Ground-floor plan.

Grundriß des Erdgeschosses.

Plan du rez-de-chaussée.

1 patio
2 guest's room
3 bathroom
4 dining room & bar
5 kitchen
6 store
7 toilet
8 yard

9 maid's room
10 car porch
11 living room
12 linkway
13 familiy room
   pavilion with master bedroom
   suite above

Top: The 2-storey pavilion with the family room at ground level and the master bedroom above.

Oben: Der zweistöckige Pavillon mit dem Gemeinschaftsraum im Erdgeschoß und dem darüber liegenden Hauptschlafzimmer.

Ci-dessus: La maison de deux étages avec la pièce familiale au rez-de-chaussée et la chambre à coucher du maître au-dessus.

The residential pavilion and court.

Der Wohnpavillon mit dem Hof.

Vue de la résidence et de la cour.

Raj **Rewal**
India

Raj Rewal's architecture has built upon itself over the years to become a distinctive reflection of his continuing concern with the crafting of buildings and the search for an appropriate language for an Indian architecture. It can be characterized as the exploration of two themes: the use of local materials mainly (stone, brick and concrete), and the morphology and form of the Indian imperial Mughal style. Interestingly, his work has been projected for and built overwhelmingly in the city of New Delhi. Rewal, who studied and worked in Europe, also tries to find ways to apply aspects of European modernism to the Indian context. His contribution encompasses a wide spectrum of programme while he is particularly known for his designs for institutions of higher education and large-scale projects for mass housing that use principles of past urban models of North India. Geometric planning and the use of clustering and terraces in neighbourhoods, accessed through distinctive portals, with a series of shared semi-public spaces, are hallmarks of his work.

Die Architektur Raj Rewals hat sich über die Jahre hinweg zu einer eigenwilligen Reflexion seines bleibenden Interesses an der handwerklichen Fertigung im Hausbau und der Suche nach einer angemessenen Sprache für die indische Architektur entwickelt. Ihn beschäftigen zwei Themenkreise: die Verwendung von überwiegend ortsüblichen Materialien (Stein, Ziegelstein und Beton) und die Morphologie sowie die Formen des indischen, imperialen Mughal-Stils. Seine Arbeiten sind überwiegend für die Stadt New Delhi konzipiert und dort auch gebaut worden. Rewal, der in Europa studiert und gearbeitet hat, will Aspekte der europäischen Moderne für den indischen Kontext fruchtbar machen. Seine Arbeiten umfassen ein breites Spektrum, besonders bekannt ist er für seine Entwürfe von universitären Einrichtungen und seine Projekte für groß angelegte Wohnsiedlungen, bei denen er sich der Konstruktionsprinzipien nordindischer Stadtmodelle bedient. Der geometrische Grundriß, die gruppenartigen Anordnungen und Terrassen in den Wohnvierteln sowie eine Anzahl von gemeinschaftlichen, halb-öffentlichen Räumen sind die Kennzeichen seiner Arbeit.

Le style de Raj Rewal s'est formé au fil des années. Il exprime une préoccupation constante qui est celle de l'exécution concrète du bâtiment et de la recherche d'un langage approprié à une architecture indienne. Deux thèmes dominent: l'utilisation de matériaux locaux (pierre, brique et béton) et la morphologie et la forme du style moghol. L'intéressant, c'est que ses projets architecturaux ont été conçus et réalisés en majeure partie à New Delhi. Rewal, qui a étudié et travaillé en Europe, essaie aussi d'appliquer certains aspects du modernisme européen au contexte indien. Son œuvre est multiple, et il est bien connu pour ses plans d'universités et ses grands ensembles d'habitations qui reprennent les principes des anciens modèles urbains de l'Inde septentrionale. Les traits distinctifs de son œuvre sont le plan géométrique et les groupes de maisons et de terrasses formant des petits quartiers, séparés par de beaux portails et ponctués d'espaces semi-publics.

View of the students' housing cluster showing the balconies and rendered façades.

Ansicht der Studentenwohnheime mit den Balkonen.

Vue de la résidence universitaire, avec ses balcons et ses façades sobres et rigoureuses.

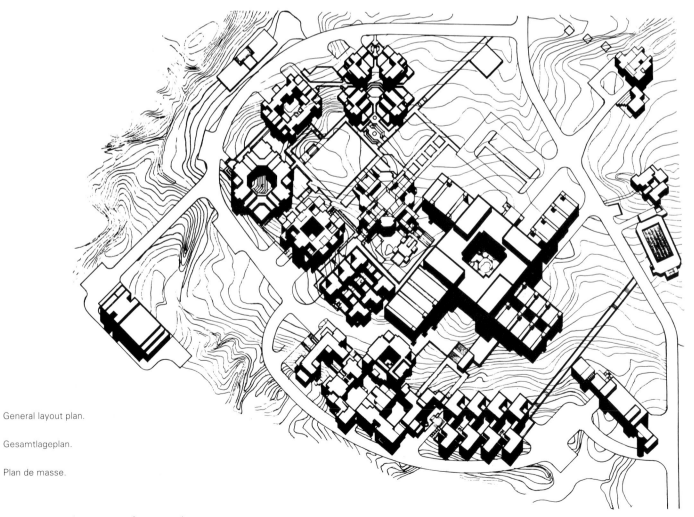

General layout plan.

Gesamtlageplan.

Plan de masse.

National Institute of Immunology (1984–90), New Delhi

The Institute is a complex of academic, laboratory, and research buildings, with five clusters of professors' and students housing, all grouped in the manner of an urban settlement. Arranged around courtyards of different sizes, the buildings are interlinked by gateways and shaded paths that offer distant vistas and changing views resulting from shifting axes. The concrete frame structure is clad with sandstone grit panels applied in situ. The colours of stone, red or beige, define the structure of the complex and echo the natural landscape.

Das Institut besteht aus Lehr-, Labor- und Forschungsgebäuden, mit fünf Einzelkomplexen, zur Unterbringung von Professoren und Studenten, die durchweg im Stil einer städtischen Siedlung angelegt sind. Die Gebäude gruppieren sich um unterschiedlich große Innenhöfe und sind miteinander durch Tore und schattige Wege verbunden, so daß durch die ständig sich verschiebenden Achsen weitreichende Durchblicke und wechselnde Aussichten geboten werden. Der Betonbau ist mit Kies-Sandstein-Platten verkleidet, die vor Ort angebracht werden. Die Farben der Steine, rot und beige, geben dem Bau seine Struktur und korrespondieren mit der natürlichen Umgebung.

L'institut comprend plusieurs bâtiments d'enseignement, de recherche et de laboratoires, ainsi qu'un ensemble de cinq résidences pour les professeurs et les étudiants, toutes regroupées à la manière d'un habitat urbain. Les constructions sont disposées autour de cours de taille différente et reliées entre elles par des portes et des allées ombragées qui créent autant de perspectives et de points de vue. L'ossature en béton est revêtue de panneaux de grès appliqués in situ. Les tons de la pierre, rouge ou beige, définissent la structure du complexe et répondent en écho au paysage naturel.

The buildings are connected through a system of walkways, gardens and courtyards, each of which is different in character and yet united through the use of the same materials.

Die einzelnen Gebäude sind durch ein System von Gehwegen, Gärten und Innenhöfen unterschiedlicher Art miteinander verbunden; durch die Verwendung der gleichen Materialien werden sie jedoch zu einer Einheit.

Les immeubles sont reliés par un système de passages, de cours et de jardins. Tous sont différents de par leur caractère, et pourtant, unis par l'emploi des mêmes matériaux.

World Bank Office (1993), New Delhi

Set in the Lodhi Estate area of the city, the building is a landmark of contemporary Indian architecture, reflecting the classical axial symmetry of the historic Lodhi architecture. Arranged around a central courtyard, the public entrance is to the east whilst the west façade is flanked by a sunken garden. The walls are of beige-coloured limestone with a ribbon of pale pink Agra stone. Careful detailing elegantly modulates a building that is both aesthetically pleasing and functionally efficient.

Das Gebäude liegt im Stadtgebiet Lodhi Estate und stellt einen Meilenstein der zeitgenössischen indischen Architektur dar, denn es spiegelt die klassische Achsensymmetrie der historischen Bauten Lodhis wider. Um einen zentralen Innenhof herum angelegt, öffnet sich der Eingang für das Publikum zum Osten hin, während die westliche Fassade von einem tiefer gelegenen Garten umgeben wird. Die Wände sind aus beigefarbenem Kalkstein, in den ein Streifen von blass-rosa Agra-Stein eingelegt ist. Die sorgfältige Ausführung der Details gibt dem Gebäude ein elegantes Aussehen; der Bau ist sowohl ästhetisch ansprechend wie auch in funktionaler Hinsicht effizient.

Construit dans le secteur du Lodhi Estate, cet immeuble est un événement marquant de l'architecture indienne contemporaine. Il reprend en effet la symétrie axiale classique de l'architecture Lohdi. L'entrée du public donne à l'est sur une cour centrale alors que la façade ouest est flanquée d'un jardin en contrebas. Les murs sont en calcaire beige agrémenté d'un bandeau de pierre d'Agra rose. Les détails soignés modulent élégamment cet immeuble à la fois esthétique et fonctionnel.

The central courtyard.

Der zentrale Innenhof.

La Cour centrale.

Entrance lobby looking towards the interior courtyard.

Eingangshalle zum Innenhof hin.

Le hall d'entrée donne sur la cour intérieure.

The building seen from the sunken garden and gardens to the west.

Blick auf das Gebäude vom Garten aus.

La banque vue depuis le jardin encaissé et les jardins à l'ouest.

The sunken garden seen from the bank offices.

Blick aus den Büroräumen der Bank auf den tiefer gelegenen Garten.

Vue du jardin encaissé depuis les bureaux de la banque.

SBA – Rasem Badran
Jordan

Principal of SBA (formerly Shubeilat Badran & Keilany), Rasem Badran is among the most interesting and significant Arab architects practising today. He was educated in Germany and worked there until his return to Amman in 1973. His firm (started 1976) has projects all over the Middle East and in Spain and Malaysia. Badran has won many architectural competitions, and his prolific out put varies from houses and housing, to universities and large institutional complexes. He uses sketches and models rather than words to express his ideas, in an intuitive rather than intellectual approach to architecture. He seeks to develop an "Islamic architecture" and a contemporary Arab architectural language, reflected in his use of the indigenous desert vernacular and in his references to past historic models. Simultaneously, he is conscious of new technological developments and integrates these into his designs.
He is also concerned with urban form and its relationship to historic Islamic cities.

Der Leiter von SBA (ehemals Shubeilat Badran & Keilany), Rasem Badran, gehört zu den bedeutendsten Architekten Arabiens. Er wurde in Deutschland ausgebildet und hat dort, bis zu seiner Rückkehr nach Amman im Jahre 1973, gearbeitet. Sein (1976 eröffnetes) Büro führt Projekte im gesamten Gebiet des Nahen Ostens durch, und in Spanien und Malaysia hat Badran zahlreiche Architektur-Wettbewerbe gewonnen. Die Palette seines Schaffens erstreckt sich von Haus- und Wohnungsbauten, über Universitäten, bis hin zu großen behördlichen Baukomplexen. Um seine Vorstellungen zum Ausdruck zu bringen, verwendet er eher Skizzen und Modelle als Worte, und bei seinen Entwürfen geht er eher intuitiv vor. Er arbeitet an der Entwicklung einer »islamischen Architektur« und einer zeitgemäßen arabischen Architektursprache, was durch die Einbeziehung der ortstypischen Wüstenlandschaft und die Bezugnahme auf historische Modelle zum Ausdruck kommt. Zugleich integriert er neue technologische Entwicklungen in seine Entwürfe. Er befaßt sich ferner mit der Form des Städtischen und deren Verhältnis zu den historischen Städten des Islam.

Rasem Badran, directeur de SBA (anciennement Shubeilat Badran & Keilany), est un des architectes arabes les plus intéressants d'aujourd'hui. Il a étudié en Allemagne où il a travaillé jusqu'à son retour à Amman en 1973. Son agence (créée en 1976) a réalisé des projets un peu partout au Moyen-Orient, ainsi qu'en Espagne et en Malaisie. Badran a remporté de nombreux concours d'architecture et son œuvre, abondante, englobe maisons et appartements, universités et complexes institutionnels. Pour exprimer ses idées, il utilise plus volontiers le croquis et la maquette que les mots, et son approche de l'architecture est plus intuitive qu'intellectuelle. Il cherche à développer une «architecture islamique» et un langage architectural arabe contemporain, comme on peut le voir dans son usage de l'architecture du désert et dans ses références aux modèles historiques. En même temps, il suit de près les avancées technologiques et les intègre dans ses plans. Il s'intéresse aussi à la configuration urbaine et à son lien avec les villes islamiques historiques.

Architect's drawing for a competition winning housing project (1991) in Sana'a, Yemen.

Prämierte Zeichnung für den Wettbewerb eines Häuser-Projektes (1991) in Sana'a, Yemen.

Dessin primé lors d'un concours pour un project immobiler (1991) à Sana'a, Yémen.

Qasr Al-Hokm Development (1979–92), Riyadh

Qasr Al-Hokm, or Justice Palace, district is the central core of Riyadh, its development divided into three phases, of which the first two have been completed. (Phase I comprises the government administrative buildings; phase II, several squares with commercial and office facilities, a large mosque, and the Justice Palace itself.) Badran's buildings interpret Najd architecture in yellow stone-clad concrete. To the south, Qasr Al-Hokm has six levels in the form of a fortress with thick walls and large towers, while the northern portion has a dramatic façade with few openings and is inwardly focused on courtyards. This complex is the most assured and authoritative of Badran's works.

Der Bezirk mit dem Qasr Al-Hokm, dem Justizpalast, bildet das Herzstück von Riyadh; seine Entwicklung umfaßte drei Phasen, von denen zwei Phasen abgeschlossen sind. (Die Phasen I und II betrafen die Verwaltungsgebäude der Regierung und die verschiedenen Plätze mit ihren kommerziellen Einrichtungen und Büroräumen, eine große Moschee und den Justizpalast selbst.) Badrans Bauten stellen eine Interpretation der Najd Architektur in mit gelbem Stein verkleideten Beton dar. Zum Süden hin ist der Qasr Al-Hokm auf sechs Ebenen in Form einer Festung angelegt, mit dicken Wänden und großen Türmen, während der nördliche Teil, der eine imposante Fassade mit wenigen Öffnungen aufweist, nach innen auf die Höfe gerichtet ist.

Le quartier de Qasr Al-Hokm, ou Palais de Justice, se trouve au cœur de Riyad. Son aménagement s'est déroulé en trois phases dont les deux premières ont été achevées (la phase I comprend les immeubles gouvernementaux, la phase II plusieurs places avec des centres commerciaux et des bureaux, une grande mosquée et le Palais de Justice). Les constructions de Badran interprètent l'architecture Najd dans un béton habillé de pierre jaune. Qasr Al-Hokm apparaît au sud comme une forteresse à six niveaux, avec des murs épais et des tours robustes. La partie nord, tournée vers les jardins, présente aux passants une impressionnante façade percée de rares ouvertures.

The approach to the audience chamber makes a powerful statement in the sequence of marble-clad columns that glow under the artificial lighting.

Der Gang zu dem Audienzzimmer inmitten einer Reihe von marmorverkleideten Säulen, die unter der künstlichen Beleuchtung erstrahlen, ist kraftvoll in seiner Aussage.

Une succession de colonnes en marbre luisant sous les éclairages artificiels confère à l'antichambre de la salle d'audience une puissante solennité.

Page 132: General view of the Justice Palace from the road.
Page 133 bottom: Entrance level of the Justice Palace containing the *majlis,* or audience halls, and government offices.

Seite 132: Gesamtansicht des Justizpalastes, von der Straße aus gesehen.
Seite 133 unten: Eingangsebene des Justizpalastes, auf der die *majlis,* oder Audienzhallen, und die Regierungsbüros liegen.

Page 132: Vue d'ensemble du Palais de Justice depuis la route.
Page 133 en bas: Niveau de l'entrée du Palais de Justice comprenant les *majlis* – les salles d'audience – et les bureaux du Gouvernement.

One of the entrances to the Justice Palace.

Einer der Eingänge des Justizpalastes.

Vue d'une des entrées du Palais de Justice.

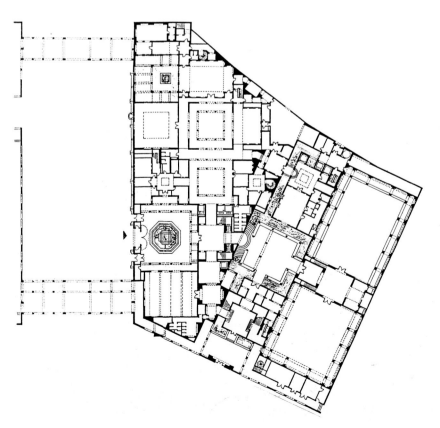

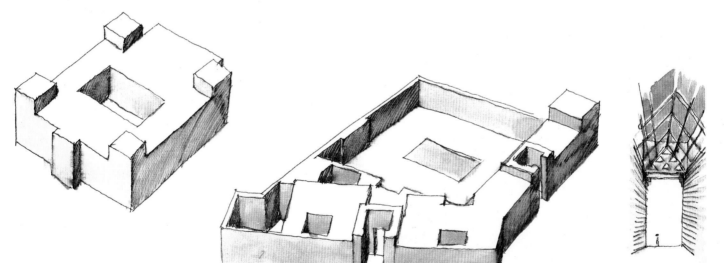

Badran develops his projects by producing hundreds of sketches. Shown here are studies for Qasr Al-Hokm.
Page 134: Interior of the mosque.

Badran entwickelt seine Projekte, indem er Hunderte von Skizzen macht. Hier abgebildet sind Studien für Qasr Al-Hokm.
Seite 134: Innenansicht der Moschee.

Badran élabore ses projets au moyen de centaines de croquis. Les études ici présentées sont celles du projet de Qasr Al-Hokm.
Page 134: L'intérieur de la mosquée.

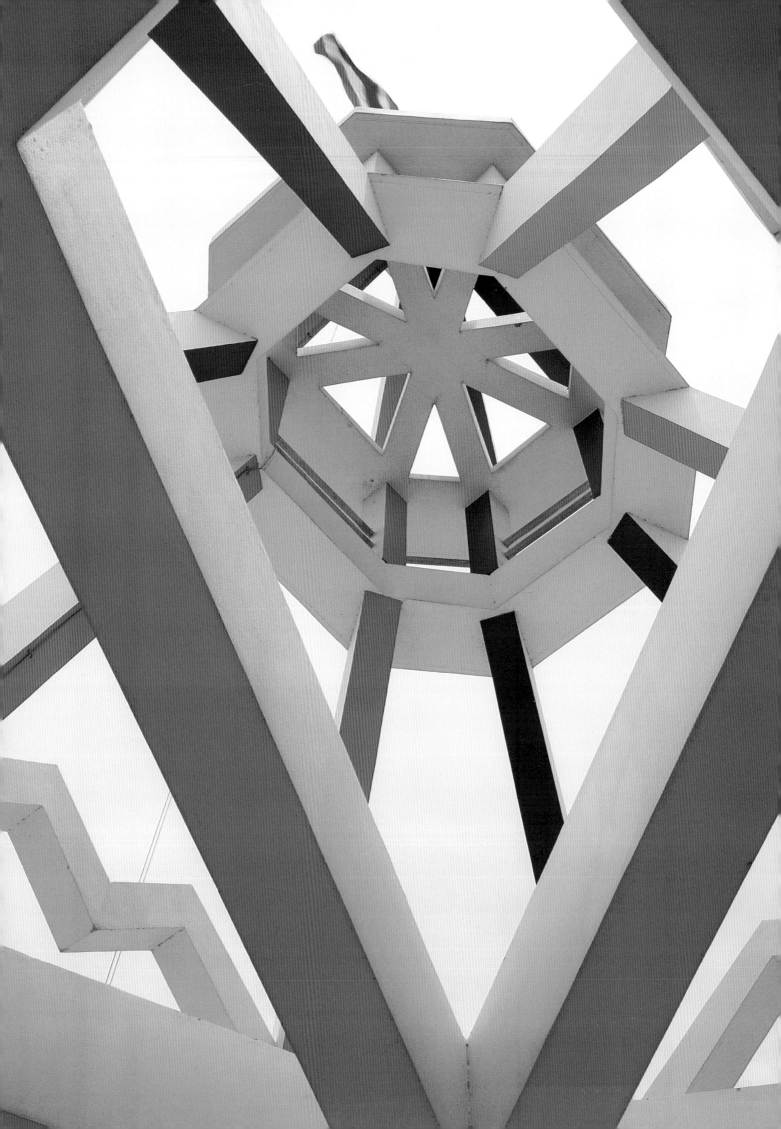

SJA + 3D
Thailand

Architect, theoretician, and writer Sumet Jumsai is an enthusiastic promoter of South-east Asia through his writings, teachings, and regular column in the Thai newspaper *Nation*. One of the most intellectual modernist architects, Jumsai was influenced in his earlier work by Le Corbusier, Colin Rowe, and Buckminster Fuller, applying contemporary European forms and technical innovations to buildings designed in the Thai context. His forward-looking attitude led him during the 1980s to a high-tech aesthetic and a theory of "robot architecture" in which the robot is seen not as a machine but as a symbol of the inseparability and interaction between machines and human beings. This was expressed most controversially in the Bank of Asia and refined in the Nation Building, both in Bangkok. More recently, he has become increasingly concerned with the vernacular context of his work, turning his attention to South-east Asian traditions of water-borne architecture and more traditional building profiles and in exploring the co-existence of industrial technology and craftsmanship within one building.

Als Architekt, Theoretiker und Schriftsteller ist Sumet Jumsai zu einem enthusiastischen Förderer Südostasiens geworden. Jumsai zählt zu den intellektuellsten modernistischen Architekten und hat sich in seinen früheren Werken von Le Corbusier, Colin Rowe und Buckminster Fuller beeinflussen lassen, indem er zeitgenössische europäische Formen und technische Innovationen verwendete. Sein in die Zukunft gerichtetes Denken brachte ihn während der achtziger Jahre mit der Ästhetik des high-tech und der Theorie der »Roboter-Architektur« in Berührung, in der der Roboter nicht als Maschine, sondern als ein Symbol der Untrennbarkeit und der Interaktion von Mensch und Maschine betrachtet wird. Dies kam in der Bank of Asia auf höchst umstrittene Art zum Ausdruck und zeigte sich im Nation Building in noch verfeinerter Form, beide in Bangkok. In jüngerer Zeit beschäftigte er sich zunehmend mit dem lokalen Kontext seiner Arbeiten, den südostasiatischen Traditionen des Wasserbaus und den traditionellen Bauformen sowie dem Nebeneinander von industrieller Technologie und Handwerkskunst innerhalb ein und desselben Gebäudes.

Jumsai compte parmi les architectes modernistes intellectuels; ses premières réalisations portent encore l'empreinte de Le Corbusier, de Colin Rowe et de Buckminster Fuller; il appliquait en effet des formes et des innovations techniques européennes à des constructions conçues dans le contexte thaï. Sa manière de voir résolument progressiste le pousse durant les années 80 vers une esthétique high-tech et la théorie de «l'architecture robot», qui voit dans le robot non une simple machine mais le symbole de l'interaction indissociable de la machine et de l'homme. Jumsai a appliqué la théorie assez brutalement dans la Banque of Asia puis, de manière plus raffinée, dans le Nation Building construits tous deux à Bangkok. Aujourd'hui, il s'intéresse de plus en plus au contexte vernaculaire de son travail, à l'architecture des maisons flottantes traditionnelles dans le Sud-Est asiatique, et aux formes de construction encore plus traditionnelles; il explore aussi les possibilités de coexistence de la technologie industrielle et de l'artisanat dans un même bâtiment.

Thammasat University (1986), Rangsit, the cut-out profile of the spire.

Thammasat University (1986), Rangsit, Blick in den Turm.

Thammasat University (1986), Rangsit, profil en coupe de la flèche.

Thammasat University (Phase I, 1986), Rangsit

The master plan for the Rangsit campus to the north of Bangkok was prepared by Jumsai in 1984 and, for its first phase, SJA designed five of its buildings: the DOM, or central administrative building, the central lecture building, the library, an audio-visual building and an academic and training centre. All the buildings are based on a square with an internal courtyard and a basic column grid of 7.8 meters. Most of them are raised on stilts above ground or water and are unified by prominent roofs and eaves, which lend a traditional character to the ensemble.

Der Gesamtplan für den Rangsit Campus im Norden Bangkoks wurde von Jumsai im Jahre 1984 erstellt, und für die erste Phase entwarf SJA fünf der Bauten – den DOM oder das zentrale Verwaltungsgebäude, das zentrale Vorlesungsgebäude, die Bibliothek, ein Gebäude für audio-visuelle Vorführungen und ein Lehr- und Ausbildungszentrum. Alle Gebäude basieren auf einer quadratischen Fläche mit einem Innenhof und einer gleichmäßigen Anordnung von 7,8 m hohen Säulen. Die meisten dieser Bauten sind auf Pfählen über dem Boden oder dem Wasser errichtet und sind durch die vorspringenden Dächer und Dachgesimse, die dem Ensemble ein traditionelles Aussehen verleihen, miteinander verbunden.

Jumsai a conçu en 1984 le plan de masse du campus de Rangsit situé au nord de Bangkok, et c'est l'agence SJA qui a dessiné les cinq bâtiments prévus dans la première phase: les bureaux de l'administration ou DOM, le bâtiment des salles de cours, la bibliothèque, un centre audiovisuel et un autre pour la formation et l'enseignement. Toutes ces constructions sont basées sur un carré avec cour intérieure et sur une grille de base de 7,8 m pour les colonnes. La plupart des bâtiments reposent sur des pilotis en surface du sol ou sur l'eau. De grands toits à auvents, qui rappellent l'architecture traditionelle, donnent à l'ensemble une belle unité.

Site plan of the area designed by SJA + 3D.

Lageplan, entworfen von SJA + 3D.

Plan de situation par SJA + 3D.

Site Plan

1. *Administrative Building*
2. *Central Lecture Building*
3. *Library*
4. *Academic Research & Training Centre*
5. *Audio Visual Centre*
6. *Parking*
7. *Pavilion*
8. *Covered walkway*
9. *Bicycle path*
10. *Gardens*

Page 138: The central administration building with its spire functioning as a landmark for the university, seen from the front lotus pond to the north.

Seite 138: Blick von dem vorderen Lotusblütenteich im Norden auf das zentrale Verwaltungsgebäude mit seinem spitz zulaufenden Turm, dem Wahrzeichen der Universität.

Page 138: Le bâtiment administratif et sa flèche, qui sert de point de repère, vus depuis le bassin aux lotus au nord.

Robot Building – Bank of Asia (1986), Bangkok

Built as a witty and controversial gesture in the urban landscape, the Bank of Asia, better known as the Robot Building, has become a city landmark with its uncompromising imagery. Although the design is humourous, it is a serious response to the programme, in which each element, such as the "eyes" and the "nuts", has practical functions, and illustrates Jumsai's view of the robot, not as a machine but as a stylized body wrapped in a high-tech skin.

Als eine ebenso witzige wie umstrittene Geste in die städtische Landschaft gesetzt, ist die Bank of Asia, besser bekannt unter dem Namen Robot Building, mit ihrer klaren, bildlichen Sprache zu einem Wahrzeichen der Stadt geworden. Bei allem Humor, der in dem Entwurf steckt, ist er doch die ernsthafte Umsetzung eines Programms, bei dem jedes Element, wie beispielsweise die »Augen« oder die »Schraubenmuttern«, tatsächlich eine praktische Funktion hat. Daß für Jumsai der Roboter keine Maschine ist, sondern eher ein stilisierter Körper, umgeben von einer High-Tech-Hülle, wird hier anschaulich dargestellt.

La Bank of Asia se voulait un clin d'œil architectural dans le paysage urbain. Très controversé au moment de sa construction, l'édifice est aujourd'hui un monument incontournable de Bangkok. Son humour et son imagerie radicale ne l'empêchent toutefois pas d'avoir un propos plus sérieux: chaque «œil», chaque écrou à une fonction bien précise. Jumsai entend démontrer ici que le robot n'est pas une machine mais corps stylisé revêtu d'une enveloppe high-tech.

The interior of the banking hall with its machine-aesthetic columns.

Der Innenraum der Bankhalle mit den von einer Maschinenästhetik geprägten Säulen.

L'intérieur de la banque avec ses colonnes évoquant des machines.

Page 141: View from the main road at night.

Seite 141: Ansicht von der Hauptstraße aus, bei Nacht.

Page 141: Vue nocturne du bâtiment depuis la rue principale.

General view of the Bay View aparte-
ments (1987), Hong Kong.

Gesamtansicht der Bay View Appartements (1987) in Hongkong.

Vue d'ensemble des appartements de
Bay View (1987), à Hong Kong.

TAOHO Design
Hong Kong

Tao Ho has a background in philosophy, music, art, and architecture and straddles the cultures of East and West. Born in Shanghai, he has lived in Canton and Hong Kong and was educated in the USA as both an architect and art historian. His work combines a number of artistic endeavours; his architecture, most influenced by Walter Gropius (with whom he worked) and Buckminster Fuller, reflects the concerns of the Modern Movement and the International Style. Since the late 1980s, when he became involved in projects in the People's Republic of China, his work has been tempered by an interest in the vernacular of the country's southern regions. After a hiatus of over twenty years, he started painting and exhibiting again, in Europe and Asia. Tao Ho's work, which has responded to the imperatives of the commercialism of Hong Kong, is beginning to change in ways that are yet to define a "new" style – but like the man himself, his experiments are always interesting.

Tao Ho kommt von der Philosophie, der Musik, der Kunst und Architektur her und ist mit den Kulturen des Osten und des Westens gleichermaßen vertraut. Er ist in Shanghai geboren, hat in Kanton und Hongkong gelebt und erhielt seine Ausbildung als Architekt und Kunsthistoriker in den USA. Am stärksten ist seine Architektur von Walter Gropius (mit dem er zusammengearbeitet hat) und Buckminster Fuller geprägt, und es spiegeln sich in ihr die Anliegen der Moderne und des »International Style«. Seit dem Ende der achtziger Jahre, als er an einigen Projekten in der Volksrepublik China beteiligt war, lassen seine Arbeiten auch das Interesse an dem einheimischen Baustil der südlichen Regionen des Landes erkennen. Nach einer Pause von mehr als zwanzig Jahren fing er erneut an zu malen und auszustellen, in Europa und Asien. Tao Hos Bauten, die in Hongkong unter dem Imperativ des Kommmerziellen standen, beginnen sich in einer Weise zu verändern, die sich erst noch zu einem »neuen« Stil herauskristallisieren muß. Aber wie der Mann selbst, sind auch seine Experimente stets interessant.

Tao Ho a une formation philosophique, musicale, artistique et architecturale et se trouve à cheval sur les cultures occidentale et asiatique. Né à Shanghaï, il a vécu à Canton et à Hong Kong, puis a étudié l'architecture et l'histoire aux Etats-Unis. Son œuvre conjuque plusieurs démarches artistiques. Son architecture, qui doit beaucoup à Walter Gropius (avec qui il travailla) et à Buckminster Fuller, exprime les mêmes préoccupations que le Mouvement moderne et le Style International. Depuis la fin des années 80, Tao Ho, chargé de divers projets en Chine, s'intéresse à l'architecture vernaculaire des régions méridionales du pays. Il a recommencé à peindre et à exposer en Europe et en Asie, après une pause de vingt années. Son œuvre, naguère soumise aux exigences de ses clients de Hong Kong, commence à changer dans le sens d'un «nouveau» style – mais les expériences sont à l'image de l'homme: toujours passionnantes.

AJ Universal Commercial Centre (1994 project), Suzhou

Located in the heart of the old city of Suzhou (the "Venice of the East", though it pre-dates Venice by 1000 years), China, is the project for a mixed-use shopping, recreational, commercial and residential complex. The 7-storey structure consists of units juxtaposed to resemble a traditional cluster of buildings, an image that is reinforced by the sloping tiled roofs. This project marks a departure in the architect's modernist work, by referring explicitly to "classical" Chinese architectural forms.

Im Herzen der alten chineschen Stadt Suzhou (dem »Venedig des Ostens«, wenngleich die Stadt bereits 1000 Jahre vor Venedig existiert hat), befindet sich ein multi-funktionales Einkaufs- und Freizeitzentrum, das aus einem kommerziellen Teil und einem Wohnkomplex besteht. Der siebengeschossige Bau setzt sich aus zwanglos aneinandergereihten Baukörpern zusammen, so daß der Eindruck eines traditionellen, natürlich gewachsenen Ensembles von Gebäuden entsteht, ein Bild, das durch die sanft geschwungenen Ziegeldächer noch verstärkt wird. Dieses Projekt symbolisiert einen Aufbruch innerhalb der modernistischen Arbeiten des Architekten, da es explizit auf die »klassischen« Formen chinesischer Architektur verweist.

Situé au cœur de la vieille ville de Suzhou (la «Venise de l'Orient», bien que née 1000 ans avant Venise), le complexe est un mélange de structures commerciales, récréatives et résidentielles. Le projet se compose de sept étages d'unités juxtaposées d'une manière qui rappelle l'habitat traditionnel, une image que les toits en pente et couverts de tuiles accentuent encore. Il marque un tournant dans le travail de l'architecte par sa référence à l'architecture chinoise classique.

Section through the building showing the seven
levels above ground and the basement retail space.
A tall atrium runs through the centre of the project.

Gebäudeschnitt mit den sieben oberirdisch gelegenen Ebenen und den Verkaufsräumen im Keller-
geschoß. Durch das Zentrum des Projektes zieht
sich ein hohes Atrium.

Vue en coupe du centre avec ses sept niveaux
et ses espaces commerciaux au sous-sol. Un
atrium s'élève au centre du complexe.

Page 144: General view of the proposed massing of
the centre.

Seite 144: Gesamtansicht des Gebäudes.

Page 144: Projet d'organisation des volumes du
centre commercial.

Roof plan of the commercial centre.

Grundriß vom Dach des Geschäftszentrums.

Plan des toits du centre commercial.

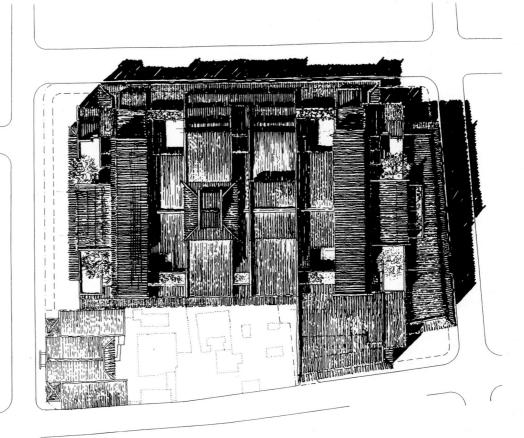

Vastu-Shilpa Consultants
India

The National Institute of Fashion Technology (1994) in New Delhi combines overlays of urban forms and the fragmentation of buildings, as a series of structures around a sunken court with the organization of an informal bazaar.

Das National Institute of Fashion Technology (1994) in New Delhi kombiniert »Überlagerungen« urbaner Formen und Fragmentierung von Bauten in einer Serie von Baukörpern um einen tiefer gelegenen Hof herum mit der lockeren Organisation eines Bazars.

Le National Institute of Fashion Technology (1994) de New Delhi: des «strates» urbaines et plusieurs bâtiments juxtaposés enserrent une cour organisée spatialement par un bazar informel.

Architect, urbanist, and educator, Balkrishna Doshi spent many years studying and travelling in Europe. His work is profoundly influenced by that of Le Corbusier (for whom he worked during the 1950s) and Louis Kahn. He has devoted his career to applying the lessons learned from the Modern Movement to the Indian context, particularly through his exploration of typologies of the city. He theorizes the city in terms of "layers" and "overlays" and is concerned predominantly with density, urban patterning, and spatial sequencing. Doshi opened his office in 1958, giving it the name Vastu-Shilpa (which means "design of environment"), and between 1977–93 he was a partner in Stein, Doshi & Bhalla. Since then, a guiding principle of his work has been to promote harmony between community and nature. Doshi plays an important role as an educator in India, and his office is a training ground for many young architects.

Note: The projects included here were done under the auspices of the firm Stein, Doshi & Bhalla.

Der Architekt, Urbanist und Pädagoge Balkrishna Doshi hat viele Jahre in Europa zugebracht, wo er studierte und reiste. Sein Werk ist stark von Le Corbusier (für den er während der fünfziger Jahre gearbeitet hat) und von Louis Kahn beeinflußt. Er hat seine berufliche Laufbahn der Anwendung der Lehren der Moderne auf den indischen Kontext gewidmet, insbesondere mit seiner Untersuchung von Stadttypologien. Er versteht die Stadt als »Schichten« und »Überlagerungen«, und er befaßt sich vor allem mit Themen wie Dichte, Stadtstrukturierung und räumliche Aufteilung. Doshi eröffnete sein Büro im Jahre 1958 unter dem Namen Vastu-Shilpa (was so viel bedeutet wie »Entwurf der Umgebung«), und zwischen 1977 und 1993 arbeitete er als Partner bei Stein Doshi & Bhalla. Seither war die Bemühung um ein harmonisches Verhältnis zwischen Gemeinschaft und Natur Leitmotiv seiner Arbeit. Als Pädagoge spielt Doshi eine wichtige Rolle in Indien; und sein Büro ist für viele junge Architekten eine Stätte der Ausbildung.

Anmerkung: Die hier vorgestellten Projekte wurden unter der Schirmherrschaft der Gruppe Stein, Doshi & Bhalla ausgeführt.

Balkrishna Doshi, architecte, urbaniste, enseignant, a passé de nombreuses années en Europe à étudier et à voyager. Il a été profondément influencé par le travail de Le Corbusier (pour qui il travailla dans les années 50) et de Louis Kahn. Il entend adapter le Mouvement moderne au contexte indien, en explorant notamment la typologie urbaine. Il décrit la ville en termes de «strates» et de «couches» et s'intéresse beaucoup aux problèmes de densité urbaine, aux modèles urbains et à l'organisation de l'espace. Doshi ouvrit son agence en 1958 et la baptisa Vastu-Shilpa («design de l'environnement»), puis il s'associa à la Stein Doshi & Bhalla, entre 1977 et 1993. Depuis, un des principes directeurs de son travail est de favoriser l'harmonie entre la communauté et la nature. Doshi joue un rôle de pédagogue en Inde, et son agence forme beaucoup de jeunes architectes.

NB: les projets présentés ici ont été réalisés sous la direction de l'agence Stein Doshi & Bhalla.

Sangath
(1981), Ahmedabad

"Sangath", which means "moving together through participation", is Doshi's own architectural office and embodies the architect's philosophy. It is set in a garden with a large pool and can be approached either through an enclosed court or by shallow steps forming an outdoor amphitheatre. The building is sunk partially below ground to present a low profile, protect it from the blistering heat, and create a terrace that modulates the spaces and connects them to the garden. Composed of vaulted interlinked structures on various levels, this dynamic building illustrates a rich blend of ideas, making it a seminal architectural work.

»Sangath« (»durch Teilnahme zusammenkommen«) ist Doshis eigenes Architekturbüro und verkörpert die Philosophie des Architekten. Es liegt inmitten eines Gartens mit einem großen Wasserbecken. Man gelangt in das Büro entweder über einen eingefriedeten Hof oder über flache Stufen, die ein Amphitheater im Freien bilden. Der Bau ist zum Teil vertieft angelegt, so daß sein Profil flach gehalten und es vor der sengenden Hitze geschützt wird. So entsteht zugleich eine Terrasse, die die Räume moduliert und sie mit dem Garten verbindet. Dieses dynamische Bauwerk, das aus gewölbten, miteinander verbundenen Bauten auf verschiedenen Ebenen besteht, illustriert eine Vielfalt von Ideen und macht es zu einem originellen Werk.

«Sangath», qui signifie «avancer ensemble par la participation», est le bureau d'architectes de Doshi et résume sa philosophie. Il est niché dans un jardin agrémenté d'une grande pièce d'eau; on peut y entrer soit par une cour fermée soit par des marches basses formant un amphithéâtre de plein air. Le bâtiment est en partie enterré, ce qui le protège de la canicule et dégage une terrasse qui module les espaces et les fait communiquer avec le jardin. Ce bâtiment dynamique, composé de structures voûtées reliées entre elles et construites à différents niveaux, témoigne d'un riche mélange d'idées qui en fait une œuvre architecturale originale et essentielle.

Page 148: The gardens, open-air "amphitheatre", and the terrace that separates the covered spaces.
Right: Architect's sketch showing the variety of heights and sections concealed under the vault.
Bottom: The vaulted interiors of the studios bring in just the right amount of natural light to produce a comfortable working environment.

Seite 148: Die Gärten, das Freiluft-»Amphitheater« und die Terrasse, die die einzelnen Baukörper voneinander trennt.
Rechts: Die Skizze des Architekten zeigt die vielen unterschiedlichen Höhen und Bereiche unter der Wölbung.
Unten: Die gewölbten Innenräume der Studios lassen genau die richtige Menge an Tageslicht herein, so daß eine angenehme Arbeitsatmosphäre entsteht.

Page 148: Les jardins, «amphithéâtre» à ciel ouvert, et la terrasse qui sépare les espaces couverts.
A droite: Croquis de l'architecte représentant les diverses hauteurs et sections dissimulées sous la voûte.
Ci-dessous: L'intérieur en voûte des ateliers laisse passer assez de lumière naturelle pour créer un agréable environnement de travail.

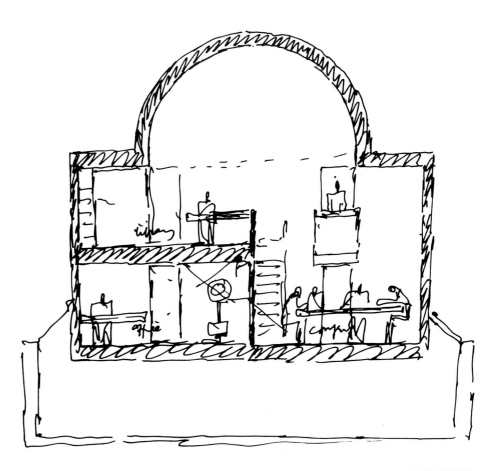

Hussain-Doshi Gufa (1993), Ahmedabad

An art gallery for the works of the noted artist M.F. Hussain, the Gufa is located on a campus of the Centre for Environmental Planning & Technology, one of Doshi's earliest works. According to Doshi, the design emerged as the result of a dream that inspired him to create a total seamless environment. The building's overlapping circular and elliptical spaces are formed under earth mounds reminiscent of cave dwellings.

Die Gufa ist eine Galerie für die Werke des bekannten Künstlers M.F. Hussain und liegt auf dem Campus des Centre for Environmental Planning & Technology (Zentrum für Umweltplanung und Technologie), das zu den Frühwerken Doshis gehört. Doshi zufolge ist der Entwurf aus einem Traum entstanden, der ihn dazu inspiriert hat, etwas zu schaffen, das vollständig mit der Umgebung verschmilzt. Die zusammenhängenden, kreisrunden und elliptischen Räume liegen unter Erdhügeln, die an Höhlenwohnungen erinnern.

La Gufa, galerie d'art consacrée aux œuvres de l'artiste M.F. Hussain, est située sur le campus du Centre for Environmental Planning & Technology, une des premières réalisations de Doshi. D'après l'architecte, c'est à la suite d'un rêve qui lui donna l'idée de créer un environnement sans césure, que le plan du bâtiment est né. Les espaces circulaires et elliptiques se déploient sous des tertres qui rappelent l'habitat préhistorique.

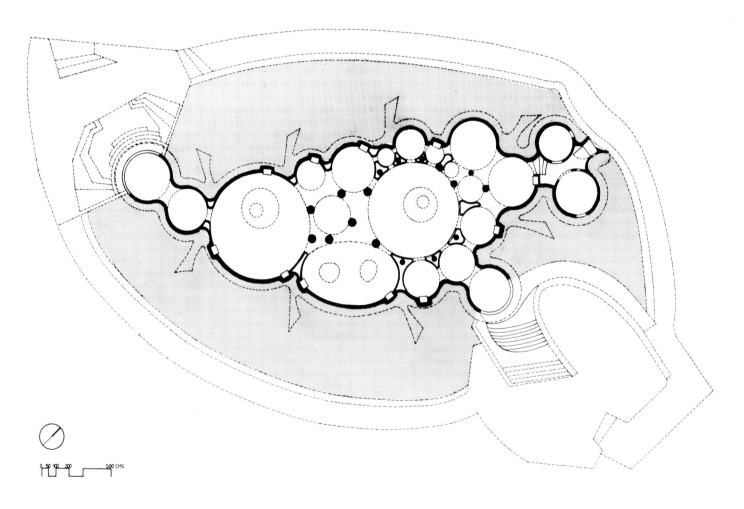

Plan of the spaces under the mound with its two structures.

Grundriß der unterhalb des Erdwalls befindlichen Räume.

Plan des différents espaces sous le tertre.

Page 151 bottom: Interior view.

Seite 151 unten: Innenansicht.

Page 151 en bas: L'espace intérieur.

Page 151 top: The ferro-cement structure is covered by a mosaic cobra drawn by the artist.

Seite 151 oben: Die Eisenzement-Konstruktion mit dem Mosaik in Form einer Kobra, das der Künstler selbst entworfen hat.

Page 151 en haut: Le béton armé de la structure décoré d'une mosaïque représentant un cobra dessinée par l'artiste.

Kyu Sung **Woo** Architect
South Korea/USA

The Kim Residence and Studio (1984–88) for an artist's family is an introverted scheme that recalls the organization (but not style) of traditional Korean houses. The artist's studio shown here is illuminated by natural light, and characterized by the architect's sense of simplicity and elegance.

Das Kim Wohnhaus und Atelier (1984–88), gebaut für eine Künstlerfamilie, hat eine nach innen ausgerichtete Struktur und erinnert an die Gliederung (aber nicht an den Stil) traditioneller koreanischer Häuser. Das hier abgebildete Atelier wird durch natürliches Licht beleuchtet und zeigt die Vorliebe des Architekten für Schlichtheit und Eleganz.

La résidence-atelier Kim (1984–88) destinée à une famille d'artiste est une structure introvertie qui rappelle l'organisation (mais non le style) de la maison coréenne traditionnelle. On voit ici l'atelier inondé de lumière naturelle. Le style sobre et élégant de l'architecte s'y exprine pleinement.

Trained in Korea and America, Kyu Sung Woo typifies the cross-cultural nature of many modern professionals. Working in both Korea and the USA, Woo participates in both societies while maintaining a critical distance. His architecture reflects a contemporary sensibility to issues of concept and detail. Woo sees his projects as evolving ideas that inform and change the built environment and, in turn, are changed by it. He establishes a dialogue with client, consultants, and colleagues to solve construction problems and form a language for the work. He believes that the specifics of site present opportunities and restrictions that should lead to solutions both particular and universal. As an urban designer, Woo understands the need to reconcile economics with functional and social needs. His firm works at extremes of scale – from the small house to mass housing and institutional buildings, all of which manifest excellence and quality.

Kyu Sung Woo wurde in Korea und Amerika ausgebildet und verkörpert den Typ des modernen, kosmopolitischen Architekten. Da Woo sowohl in Korea als auch in den USA tätig ist, nimmt er zwar an beiden Kulturen Anteil, bewahrt sich aber eine kritische Distanz. Woo sieht seine Projekte als sich entwickelnde Vorstellungen, die die bauliche Umgebung durchdringen und verändern und die ihrerseits wieder durch sie verändert werden. Er unterhält einen ständigen Dialog mit Auftraggebern, Beratern und Kollegen, um Konstruktionsprobleme zu lösen und eine dem Bauwerk angemessene Sprache zu finden. Er ist der Ansicht, daß die Besonderheiten eines Baugeländes immer zugleich Möglichkeiten und Einschränkungen mit sich bringen, für die entsprechende Lösungen gefunden werden sollten. Als Stadtplaner kennt Woo die Notwendigkeit, das Wirtschaftliche mit dem Funktionalen und den sozialen Erfordernissen in Einklang zu bringen. Seine Arbeiten umfassen das gesamte Spektrum – angefangen bei kleinen Häusern, über große Wohnkomplexe, bis hin zu den institutionellen Bauten, die durchweg von hoher Qualität sind.

Formé en Corée et en Amérique, Kyu Sung Woo représente le type même de l'architecte moderne cosmopolite. Il travaille aussi bien en Corée qu'aux Etats-Unis, et participe à la vie de deux sociétés tout en gardant une distance critique à leur égard. Son architecture exprime une sensibilité très contemporaine aux concepts et au détail. Woo voit ses réalisations comme des idées en mouvement qui transforment l'environnement bâti, et qui sont à leur tour changées par lui. Il dialogue toujours avec son client, les consultants et ses confrères pour résoudre les problèmes de construction et trouver un langage propre au projet. Pour lui, le site est à la fois une chance et une contrainte qui devraient permettre de trouver des solutions particulières et universelles. Dans son travail d'urbaniste, Woo s'efforce de concilier contraintes économiques, impératifs fonctionnels et besoins sociaux. Il est tout aussi capable de concevoir une modeste maison que des grands ensembles et des bâtiments publics. Ses réalisations sont toujours de qualité.

Olympic Village Housing (1988), Seoul

Built for the 24th Olympic Games, the project consists of 5 540 units of housing and supporting facilities located south of the city. The housing, by Woo & Williams, won an international competition in 1985. Working with Ilkum Architects, a host of consultants, and 13 major Korean contributors, the project was built within 18 months. The fan-shaped arrangement, with the tallest buildings defining the periphery, appears simple in plan but allows for a multitude of complex interior and exterior spaces. The buildings were pre-sold to individuals, who moved in after the Games to establish a permanent urban community.

Dieses Projekt, gebaut für die 24. Olympischen Spiele, besteht aus 5 540 Wohneinheiten und den dazugehörigen Einrichtungen. Mit ihren Wohnbauten gewannen Woo & Williams 1985 einen internationalen Wettbewerb. In Zusammenarbeit mit Ilkum Architects, einem als Gastgeber fungierenden Consulting Büro, und 13 Unternehmen aus Korea wurde das Projekt binnen 18 Monaten erbaut. Das fächerförmige Arrangement, dessen Silhoutte von den höchsten Gebäuden begrenzt wird, wirkt vom Grundriß her einfach, läßt jedoch eine Vielzahl komplexer innerer und äußerer Räume entstehen.

Réalisé à l'occasion des 24ᵉ jeux olympiques, le projet regroupe 5 540 logements et des annexes. Le village conçu par Woo & Williams remporta un concours international en 1985. L'agence, secondée par Ilkum Architects, des consultants et 13 grands partenaires coréens, réussit à terminer le chantier en 18 mois. Le plan en éventail semble simple, mais il donne une grande souplesse pour les aménagements intérieurs. Les immeubles avaient été vendus à l'avance à des particuliers qui y emménagèrent après les jeux.

Page 154: The U-shaped galleria at the centre of the housing project.
Right top: Housing overlooking a wide landscaped strip, which acts as an access and recreational space.
Right bottom: Aerial view of the housing scheme in a radial pattern that conforms to the bowl-shaped terrain, and is linked by a park and stream to the main complex by a U-shaped public plaza and galleria (formerly the athletes' dining hall).

Seite 154: Die U-förmige Galleria im Zentrum der Wohnanlage.
Rechts oben: Wohnbauten mit Blick auf den Garten, der als Zugangsbereich und zugleich als Erholungsraum dient.
Rechts unten: Luftbild der Wohnanlage mit ihrer strahlenförmigen Struktur, die sich der Beckenform des Terrains anpaßt. Die Wohnbauten sind durch einen Park und einen Fluß mit dem U-förmigen, öffentlichen Platz und der Galleria (früher der Speisesaal für die Sportler), dem Hauptkomplex, verbunden.

Page 154: La galerie en U au centre du projet immobiler.
Ci-dessus à droite: Les logements donnent sur des jardins aménagés tout en longueur qui servent à la fois d'accès et d'espaces de détente.
Ci-contre à droite: Vue aérienne du village olympique. Le plan a été conçu d'après la forme arrondie du site. Une place en U et une galerie (l'ancien réfectoire des athlètes) permettent d'accéder au reste du complexe.

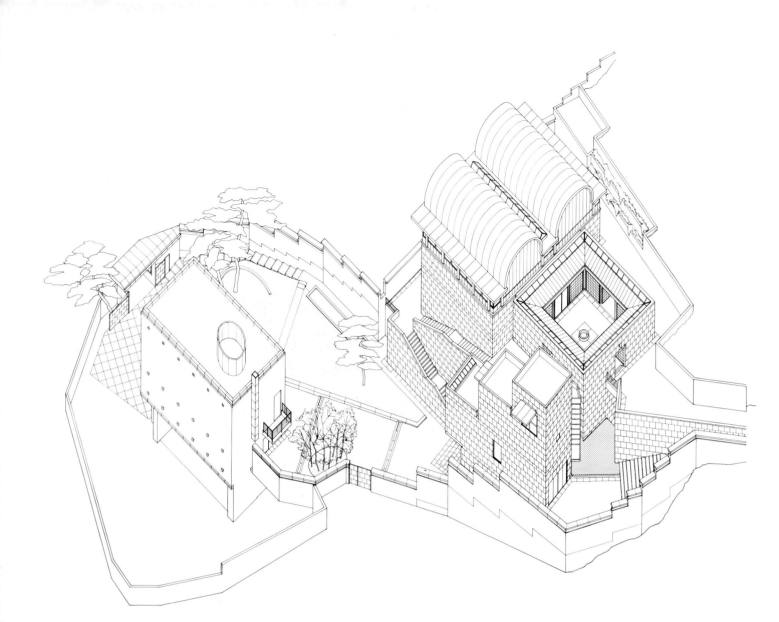

Whanki Museum (1988–93), Seoul

Dedicated to the memory of the contemporary painter Kim Whanki, the museum is set on a sloping site and conceived as a stepped complex in two blocks; the main block houses the artist's own work, while an annex houses temporary exhibition space, a cafeteria, and a shop. The steel-frame structure is faced with local granites and concrete brick, and has lead-coated copper roofs. Stone, glass blocks, and wood are used in the interiors. Grouped around a courtyard and surrounded by a compound wall, the buildings follow the east-west axis of the valley. The spaces reveal the artist's works admirably, and the lighting creates an atmosphere of quiet elegance.

Das Museum, das dem Andenken an den zeitgenössischen Maler Kim Whanki gewidmet ist, liegt an einem Hang und ist als ein gestufter Komplex mit zwei Blöcken konzipiert – der Hauptblock beherbergt die eigenen Arbeiten des Künstlers, während der andere Raum für laufende Ausstellungen, eine Cafeteria und einen Laden bietet. Die Stahlrahmenkonstruktion wurde mit örtlichem Granit und Zementsteinen verkleidet und mit einem verbleiten Kupferdach versehen. Für die Innenräume wurden Stein, Glassbausteine und Holz verwendet. Die Gebäude liegen um einen Innenhof, von einer Mauer umgeben, und folgen in ihrer Ausrichtung der Ost-West-Achse des Tales.

Ce musée consacré au peintre Kim Whanki, aujourd'hui disparu, est accroché sur plusieurs niveaux au flanc d'une colline. Le bâtiment principal abrite l'œuvre de l'artiste tandis que l'autre abrite des expositions temporaires, une cafétéria et une boutique. L'ossature en acier est revêtue de granit de la région et de briques de béton, les toits sont en cuivre recouvert de plomb. La pierre, la brique de verre et le bois forment les revêtements intérieurs. Les bâtiments, construits sur l'axe est-ouest de la vallée, sont groupés autour d'une cour et entourés d'une enceinte. Le caractère simple et fort de l'espace met en valeur les œuvres de l'artiste.

Page 156: Axonometric drawing of the museum.
Right top: Vaulted main gallery, and the studio-conservation block.

Seite 156: Axonometrische Zeichnung des Museums.
Rechts oben: Die gewölbte Hauptgalerie und die Restaurierungswerkstätten. .

Page 156: Axonométrie du musée.
A droite: La grande galerie voûtée et l'atelier de conservation de la collection.

The central gallery space below the main courtyard is lit directly from above, and indirectly through the mezzanine.

Der zentrale Raum der Galerie unterhalb des Hauptinnenhofes wird direkt von oben beleuchtet, außerdem indirekt durch das Zwischengeschoß.

La grande salle d'exposition située sous la cour principale reçoit une lumière zénithale, et elle est éclairée indirectement par la mezzanine.

Bibliography
Bibliographie

General · Allgemeines · Thèmes Généraux

Architettura nei paesi islamici: seconda mostra internazionale de architettura. Edizioni la biennale di Venezia. Venice: Electa Editrice, 1982.

"Contemporary Asian Architecture: works of APAC members" *Process Architecture,* No. 20, Nov. 1980.

Grover, Razia, ed.: *Architecture of SAARC Nations (South Asia).* New Delhi: Media Transasia, 1991.

King, Anthony D.: *Urbanism, Colonialism and the World Economy.* London: Routledge, 1990.

Kultermann, Udo: *Architekten der Dritten Welt.* Cologne: DuMont Buchverlag, 1980.

Powell, Robert, ed.: *Architecture and Identity.* Aga Khan Award for Architecture. Singapore: Concept Media, 1984.

Powell, Robert, ed.: *Regionalism in Architecture.* Aga Khan Award for Architecture. Singapore: Concept Media, 1986.

Vale, Lawrence J.: *Architecture, Power, and National Identity.* New Haven, Conn.: Yale University Press, 1992.

Country Specific · Landesspezifische Lektüre · Thèmes Spécifiques

Akihary, Huib: *Architectuur & stedebouw in Indonesie, 1870–1970.* Zutphen: De Walburg Pers, c. 1990.

Amirahmadi, Hooshang, and Salah S. El-Shakhs, eds.: *Urban Development in the Muslim World.* New Brunswick, N.J.: Center for Urban Policy Research, 1993.

Architectures en Inde (exhibition catalogue). Paris: Electa Moniteur, 1985.

Award 1991. Jakarta: Institute of Architects, 1992.

Bawa, Geoffrey, Christoph Bon, and Dominic Sansoni:
Lunuganga. Singapore: Times Editions, 1990.

Beamish, Jane, and Jane Ferguson: *A History of Singapore Architecture.* Singapore: Graham Brash, 1985.

Bhatia, Gautam: *Laurie Baker.* New Delhi: Viking, 1991.

Bhatt, Vikram, and Peter Scriver: *After the Masters: Contemporary Indian Architecture.* Ahmedabad: Mapin Publishing and Middletown, New Jersey: Grantha Corporation, 1990.

Bozdogan, Sibel, Suha Özkan, and Engin Yenal: *Sedad Eldem.* Singapore: Concept Media, 1987.

Chen Che Yoong, ed.: *Post-Merdeka Architecture, Malaysia, 1957–1987.* Kuala Lumpur: Institute of Architects of Malaysia, 1987.

Correa, Charles: *Five Projects: A Portfolio of Architecture.* India: 1992.

Correa, Charles: *The New Landscape.* A Mimar Book. London: Butterworth Architecture, 1989.

Curtis, William J. R: *Balkrishna Doshi: An Architecture for India.* Ahmedabad: Mapin Publishing, 1988.

Curtis, William J. R., and Daniel Treiber: *Raj Rewal.* Paris: Electa Moniteur, 1986.

Holod, Renata, and Ahmet Evin, eds.: *Modern Turkish Architecture.* Philadelphia: University of Pennsylvania Press, 1984.

Khan, Hasan-Uddin: *Charles Correa.* Singapore: Concept Media, 1984.

Koreana. Architecture special issue. Vol. 3, No. 3, 1989.

Lim, William S. W.: *Cities for People.* Singapore: Select Books, 1990.

Park, Sam Y.: *An Introduction to Korean Architecture.* Seoul: Jungwoo-Sa Pub. Co., 1991.

Powell, Robert: *Innovative Architecture of Singapore.* Singapore: Select Books, 1989.

Powell, Robert: *The Southeast Asian House.* Singapore: Select Books, 1991.

Talib, Kaizer: *Shelter in Saudi Arabia.* New York: St. Martin's Press, 1984.

Taylor, Brian Brace: *Raj Rewal.* London: Concept Media, 1992.

Taylor, Brian Brace: *Geoffrey Bawa.* Singapore: Concept Media, 1986.

Yeang, Ken: *The Architecture of Malaysia.* Amsterdam and Kuala Lumpur: Pepin Press, 1992.

Yeang, Ken: *Tropical Urban Regionalism.* Singapore: Concept Media, 1987.

Yilan, Gao: *Architecture in New China.* Center for Environmental Research. Berkeley, Calif.: University of California, 1987.

Photographic credits
Fotonachweis
Crédits photographiques

The publisher and editor wish to thank each of the architects and photographers for their kind assistance.

P. 2:   © Mick Hales
P. 6:   Robert L. Miller, 1989
P. 8/11:   H.U. Khan
P. 12:   K.K. Ashraf
P. 13:   S. Javed
P. 15:   H.U. Khan
P. 19:   Shezad Noorani
P. 21:   H.U. Khan
P. 22:   CDA brochure
P. 24:   H.U. Khan
P. 28:   Argun Dundar, courtesy, The Aga Khan Trust for Culture (AKTC)
P. 29:   Reha Gunay, courtesy, AKTC
P. 30:   Hassan Fathy Archives, courtesy, AKTC
P. 31:   H.U. Khan
P. 32:   Courtesy, AKTC
P. 33:   H.U. Khan
P. 34 left: The Aga Khan Program Visual Archives, MIT, John Dale/1985
P. 34 right: Courtesy, Habib Fida Ali
P. 35:   Christopher Little, courtesy, AKTC
P. 36:   Silvio Caputo
P. 37:   M. Perera
P. 38:   H.U. Khan
P. 39:   Brian B. Taylor
P. 40:   H. U. Khan
P. 41:   Courtesy, Space Group of Korea
P. 43:   Courtesy, Zo Kunyong
P. 44:   H.U. Khan, courtesy, AKTC
P. 45:   H.U. Khan
P. 48:   Courtesy, Payette Associates
P. 50:   H.U. Khan
P. 51:   Pascal Marechaux, courtesy, AKTC
P. 53:   © Paolo Giordano
P. 54:   Oruç Cakmali/1983, courtesy, *Mimar*
P. 55:   H.U. Khan
P. 56–61:   Courtesy Tay Kheng Soon
P. 62–67:   Courtesy, Adhi Moersid/Atelier 6
P. 68:   © Richard Bryant
P. 69:   Courtesy, AKTC

P. 70 top: H.U. Khan
P. 70/71 bottom: Courtesy, AKTC
P. 71 top/72:   H.U. Khan
P. 73:   Simon Laird
P. 74:   © Richard Bryant
P. 75 bottom: H.U. Khan
P. 75 top: Simon Laird
P. 76:   Hassan Gardezi
P. 77:   Courtesy, BEEAH
P. 78:   Courtesy, A. Shuaibi/BEEAH
P. 79:   Reha Gunay, courtesy, AKTC
P. 80/81:   Courtesy, A. Shuaibi/BEEAH
P. 82:   Christopher Little, Courtesy, AKTC
P. 83/84 top: Courtesy, Turgut Cansever
P. 84 bottom: Cemal Emden, courtesy, AKTC
P. 85:   Cemal Emden, courtesy, AKTC
P. 86–87:   Courtesy, C.M. Correa
P. 88 top: H.U. Khan
P. 88 bottom: Courtesy, C. M. Correa
P. 89–90:   H.U. Khan
P. 91–93:   Mahendra Singh
P. 94–95:   Courtesy, J. Lim/CSL
P. 96:   K.L. Ng, courtesy, AKTC
P. 97 top: Courtesy, J. Lim/CSL
P. 97 bottom: K.L. Ng, courtesy, AKTC
P. 98–99:   Courtesy, J. Lim/CSL
P. 100:   Hassan Gardezi
P. 101:   Courtesy, N.A. Dada
P. 102 top left and right: Hassan Gardezi
P. 102 bottom: Courtesy, N.A. Dada
P. 103–105:   Hassan Gardezi
P. 106:   Courtesy, T.R. Hamzah & Yeang
P. 107–111:   © T.R. Hamzah & Yeang
P. 112:   Jung Jung-Woong
P. 113:   Courtesy, Kim Won
P. 114–117:   Jung Jung-Woong
P. 118–123:   Courtesy, W. Lim Associates
P. 124:   Mahan Mahatta
P. 125:   Hélène Rewal
P. 126 top: Raj & Hélène Rewal
P. 126 bottom: Courtesy, R. Rewal
P. 127:   Raj & Hélène Rewal
P. 128 top: H.U. Khan
P. 128 bottom: Raj & Hélène Rewal
P. 129 top: Raj & Hélène Rewal
P. 129 bottom: Hélène Rewal
P. 130–135:   Courtesy, R. Badran/SBA
P. 136–137:   Courtesy, SJA
P. 138:   Profile

P. 139:   Courtesy, SJA
P. 140/141:   Profile
P. 142:   Sam Tse
P. 143–145:   Courtesy, Tao Ho
P. 146:   John Panikar, Courtesy, B. Doshi
P. 147:   Joan Pierpoline
P. 148:   © Paolo Giordano
P. 149 top: B. Doshi
P. 149 bottom: © Paolo Giordano
P. 150:   Courtesy, B. Doshi
P. 151 top: John Panikar
P. 151 bottom: © Paolo Giordano
P. 152:   © Mick Hales
P. 153 top: Courtesy, Kyn Sung Woo
P. 154/155 top: © Mick Hales
P. 155 bottom: Courtesy, Kyu Sung Woo
P. 156:   Courtesy, Kyu Sung Woo
P. 157:   © Timothy Hursley

Acknowledgements · Danksagung · Remerciements

First and foremost I should like to thank Kimberly Mims for her research and work on the manuscript, for her valuable suggestions, manuscript preparation, corrections and advice. Two other people are due grateful acknowledgement: John de Monchaux and Karen Longeteig, both of whom read the essay text on short notice and offered wise and helpful counsel. I approached several people for guidance on the right directions for material and for advice on architects, which they generously and willingly gave. They are Stanford Anderson and Sibel Bozdogan of MIT, Kim Ghee Wan at the Korean mission in Geneva, John K.C. Liu in Taipei, Kyu Sung Woo in Cambridge, and Yoon of AREA Architects in Seoul. I remain in admiration of their erudition and expertise, and in gratitude for their assistance. I have also had a great deal of support and encouragement from Angelika Muthesius and her colleagues at Taschen publishers, to whom I offer my thanks. The back issues of the quarterly journal *Mimar: Architecture in Development* (of which I was editor between 1981–92) and the archives of the Aga Khan Trust for Culture in Geneva proved invaluable for certain project documentation and for photographs. My acknowledgement and thanks for permission to use these materials goes to the Trust. Gratitude for crucial and timely assistance with images is due to Richard and Kelli Gutman of Slide Factor in West Roxbury, Massachusetts; to Christoph Bon and Jean Chamberlin in London, to Brian Mulder in Cambridge, to Tan Joo Heng in Singapore, Helen Yap in Kuala Lumpur, to the Aga Khan Trust for Culture librarian William O'Reilly and to Katy Poole and her student helper Aparna Datey at the MIT Rotch Library. I am very grateful to all the featured architects who went to a great deal of trouble to provide me with information and with copies of illustrative material. Without their interest and co-operation this book could not have been produced. I especially thank the following for giving me their images: they are Rasem Badran, Christoph Bon, Balkrishna Doshi, Tao Ho, Sumet Jumsai, Kim Won, Jimmy Lim, William Lim, Adhi Moersid, Milroy Perera, Raj Rewal, Ali Shuaibi, Tay Kheng Soon and Ken Yeang. Special recognition is due to Philip Jodidio of the review *Connaissance des Arts* in Paris for his friendship and encouragement, which I appreciate immensely, as well as for his introduction to the publisher!

Als erstes und vor allen Dingen möchte ich Kimberly Mims für ihre Recherchen und ihre Arbeit an dem Manuskript danken, für ihre wertvollen Anregungen und vorbereitenden Arbeiten für das Manuskript, ihre Korrekturen und Ratschläge. Zwei weiteren Menschen gebührt meine dankbare Anerkennung: John de Monchaux und Karen Longeteig, die den Text des Essays kurzfristig gelesen und mir mit klugen und hilfreichen Ratschlägen zur Seite gestanden haben. An verschiedene Leute habe ich mich bezüglich der richtigen Methode zur Beschaffung von Materialien und zur Information über die Architekten ratsuchend gewandt, wobei diese mir großzügig und gerne geholfen haben. Es handelt sich dabei um Stanford Anderson und Sibel Bozdogan vom MIT, Kim Ghee Wan von der Koreanischen Gesandtschaft in Genf, John K.C. Liu in Taipeh, Kyu Sung Woo in Cambridge und Yoon von AREA Architects in Seoul. Ich bewundere ihre hohe Bildung und Sachkenntnis und bin ihnen für ihre Hilfe sehr dankbar. Ferner habe ich große Unterstützung und Ermutigung von Angelika Muthesius und ihren Kollegen vom Taschen Verlag erhalten, denen ich dafür danke. Die zurückliegenden Ausgaben der vierteljährlich erscheinenden Zeitschrift »Mimar: Architecture in Development« (deren Herausgeber ich 1981–92 war) und die Archive des Aga Khan Trust for Culture in Genf waren für die Dokumentation bestimmter Projekte und für die Fotografien von unschätzbarem Wert. Dem Trust möchte ich meine Wertschätzung und meinen Dank dafür aussprechen, daß er mir gestattet hat, diese Materialien zu benutzen. Mein Dank geht an Richard und Kelli Gutman von Slide Factor in West Roxbury, Massachusetts; Christoph Bon und Jean Chamberlin in London, Brian Mulder in Cambridge, Tan Joo Heng in Singapur, Helen Yap in Kuala Lumpur, dem Bibliothekar William O'Reilly, vom Aga Khan Trust for Culture sowie Katy Poole und ihrer studentischen Hilfskraft Aparna Datey in der Rotch Library des MIT für die wichtige und termingerechte Bereitstellung der Bildmaterialien. Ich danke allen hier vorgestellten Architekten für die große Mühe, der sie sich unterzogen haben, um mir Informationen und Kopien ihrer Bildmaterialien zukommen zu lassen. Ohne ihr Interesse und ihr kooperatives Verhalten wäre dieses Buch nicht zustande gekommen. Ganz besonders möchte ich den folgenden Personen für die Überlassung ihrer Bilder danken: Rasem Badran, Christoph Bon, Balkrishna Doshi, Tao Ho, Sumet Jumsai, Kim Won, Jimmy Lim, William Lim, Adhi Moersid, Milroy Perera, Raj Rewal, Ali Shuaibi, Tay Kheng Soon und Ken Yeang. Ganz besonderer Dank gebührt Philip Jodidio von der Zeitschrift »Connaissance des Arts« in Paris für seine mir wertvolle Freundschaft und Ermutigung, wie auch dafür, daß er mich mit dem Verlag bekanntgemacht hat!

J'aimerais tout d'abord renouveler mes remerciements à Kimberly Mims pour ses recherches et son travail sur le manuscrit, pour ses précieuses suggestions, sa préparation du manuscrit, ses corrections et ses conseils. Des remerciements particuliers aussi à John de Monchaux et Karen Longeteig qui ont lu le texte de cet ouvrage en peu de temps et m'ont donné des conseils avisés et utiles. Ma reconnaissance s'adresse également à plusieurs personnes qui avec une grande générosité m'ont assisté dans la recherche de matériaux et m'ont conseillé sur les architectes. Parmi elles, Stanford Anderson et Sibel Bozdogan du MIT, Kim Ghee Wan de la mission coréenne à Genève, John K.C Liu de Taïpei, Kyu Sung Woo de Cambridge et Yoon de AREA Architects à Séoul. J'admire leur érudition et leur compétence et tiens à leur témoigner ma gratitude pour leur aide. Je remercie aussi Angelika Muthesius et ses collègues des éditions Taschen pour leur soutien et leurs encouragements. La revue trimestrielle «Mimar: Architecture in Development» (dont je fus le rédacteur en chef de 1981 à 1992) et les archives du Aga Khan Trust for Culture à Genève m'ont été d'une aide inestimable pour la recherche iconographique et documentaire. Ma reconnaissance et mes remerciements s'adressent au Trust pour m'avoir permis d'utiliser ces matériaux. Toute ma gratitude à Richard et Kelli Gutman de Slide Factor à West Roxbury, Massachusetts, à Christoph Bon et Jean Chamberlin, Londres, à Brian Mulder, Cambridge, à Tan Joo Heng, Singapour, Helen Yap, Kuala Lumpur, à William O'Reilly, bibliothécaire de l'Aga Khan Trust for Culture, et enfin à Katy Poole et Aparna Datey, son assistante, du MIT Rotch Library pour leur assistance lors de la recherche iconographique. Je tiens à témoigner ma reconnaissance à tous les architectes figurant dans cet ouvrage qui se sont donné beaucoup de peine pour me fournir des informations et des copies de certaines illustrations. Ce livre n'aurait pu être publié sans leur intérêt et leur aimable collaboration. Je remercie tout particulièrement Rasem Badran, Christoph Bon, Balkrishna Doshi, Tao Ho, Sumet Jumsai, Kim Won, Jimmy Lim, William Lim, Adhi Moersid, Milroy Perera, Raj Rewal, Ali Shuaibi, Tay Kheng Soon et Ken Yeang pour m'avoir donné leurs photos. Que Philip Jodidio de la revue «Connaissance des Arts» de Paris soit remercié pour son amitié et son aide dans les premiers contacts avec l'éditeur.